LANGUAGE!®

The Comprehensive Literacy Curriculum

Reading
Writing
Spelling
Vocabulary
Grammar
Speaking

Jane Fell Greene, Ed.D.

Cambium LEARNING® Group | Voyager LEARNING

12 13 14 15 16   BNG   20 19 18 17 16

Authors:
Jane Fell Greene, Ed.D.
Nancy Chapel Eberhardt

The Duke Ellington Orchestra is a registered trademark of the Estate of Mercer K. Ellington. Graceland is a registered trademark of Elvis Presley Enterprises, Inc. Grammy is a registered trademark of the National Academy of Recording Arts and Sciences, Inc. Newport Jazz Festival is a registered trademark of Festival Productions. Project Exploration is a registered trademark of Project Exploration Not-For-Profit Corporation.

For acknowledgments of permissioned material, See Sources, page 190.

ISBN 13: 978-1-60218-663-7
ISBN 10: 1-60218-663-4
169076

Printed in the United States of America

Published and distributed by

17855 Dallas Parkway, Suite 400 • Dallas, TX 75287 • 800 547-6747
www.voyagerlearning.com

Table of Contents • Handbook

Table of Contents • Handbook

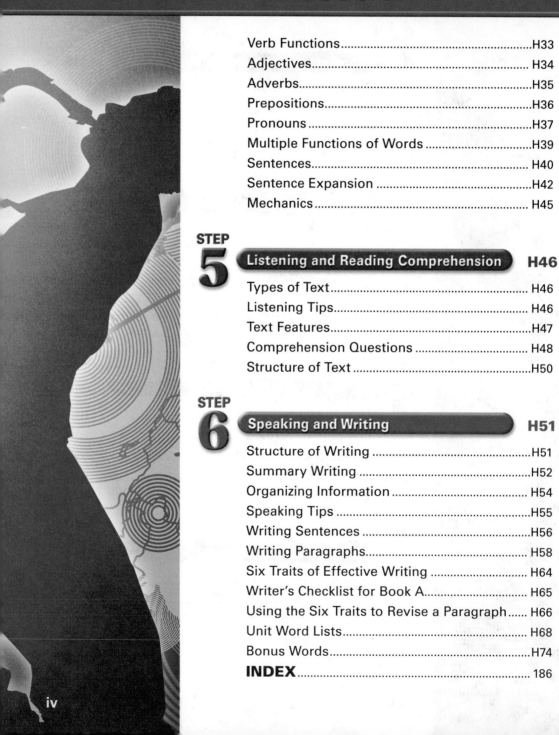

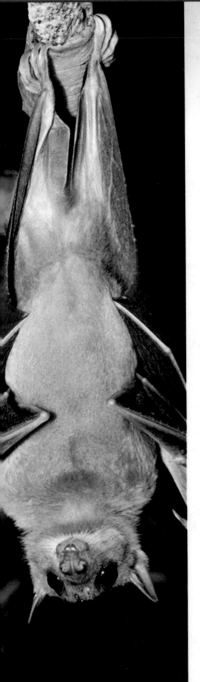

v

Unit 3

Dig It !

Decodable
Build Knowledge
Fluency

Instructional
Use Text Features
Predict
Build Knowledge
Build Vocabulary
Clarify Meaning
Apply Vocabulary

Challenge
Build Knowledge
Build Vocabulary
Clarify Meaning

Unit 4
Twins Together

Decodable
Build Knowledge
Fluency

Instructional
Use Text Features
Predict
Build Knowledge
Build Vocabulary
Clarify Meaning
Apply Vocabulary

Challenge
Build Knowledge
Build Vocabulary
Clarify Meaning

Unit 5

Jazz It Up

Decodable
Build Knowledge
Fluency

Instructional
Use Text Features
Predict
Build Knowledge
Build Vocabulary
Clarify Meaning
Apply Vocabulary

Challenge
Build Knowledge
Build Vocabulary
Clarify Meaning

Unit

6

It's Toxic

Decodable
Build Knowledge
Fluency

Instructional
Use Text Features
Predict
Build Knowledge
Build Vocabulary
Clarify Meaning
Apply Vocabulary

Challenge
Build Knowledge
Build Vocabulary
Clarify Meaning

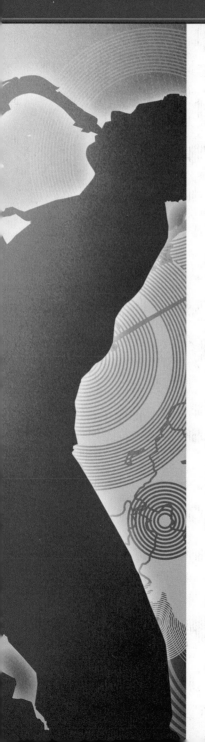

Table of Contents • Resources

Handbook

Handbook

How to use a Table of Contents and an Index

To find information in this Handbook, you can use the Handbook Table of Contents, pages iii–iv, or the Handbook Index, pages 186–189. Below are some tips for using both features.

Table of Contents

A table of contents lists **general** topics in the order they are presented in a book. Use a table of contents when you are looking for a general topic.

Index

An index lists **specific** topics in alphabetical order.

Use an index when you are looking for a specific topic.

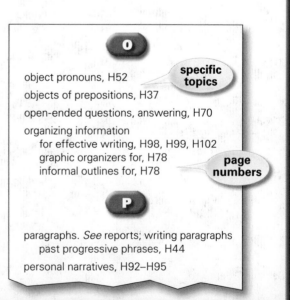

STEP 1

Phonemic Awareness and Phonics

Consonants and Vowels (Unit 1)

Languages have two kinds of sounds: **consonants** and **vowels**.

- **Consonants** are closed sounds. They restrict or close the airflow using the lips, teeth, or tongue.

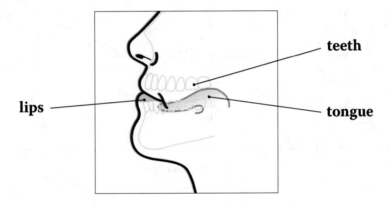

- **Vowels** are open sounds. The air doesn't stop.

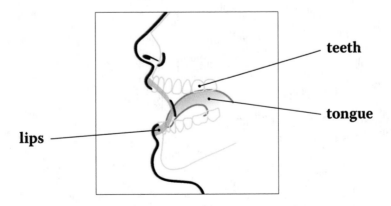

English Consonant Chart

(Note the voiceless/voiced consonant phoneme pairs)

Mouth Position

Type of Consonant Sound		Lips (Bilabial)	Lips/Teeth (Labiodental)	Tongue Between Teeth (Dental)	Tongue Behind Teeth (Alveolar)	Roof of Mouth (Palatal)	Back of Mouth (Velar)	Throat (Glottal)
	Stops	/p/ /b/			/t/ /d/		/k/ /g/	
	Fricatives		/f/ /v/	/th/ /<u>th</u>/	/s/ /z/	/sh/ /zh/		/h/[1]
	Affricatives					/ch/ /j/		
	Nasals	/m/			/n/		/ng/	
	Lateral				/l/			
	Semivowels	/ʰw/ /w/[2]			/r/	/y/		

1 Classed as a fricative on the basis of acoustic effect. It is like a vowel without voice.

2 /ʰw/ and /w/ are velar as well as bilabial, as the back of the tongue is raised as it is for /u/.

English Consonant Chart based on Bolinger, D. 1975. *Aspects of Language* (2nd ed.). Harcourt Brace Jovanovich, p. 41.

English Vowel Chart

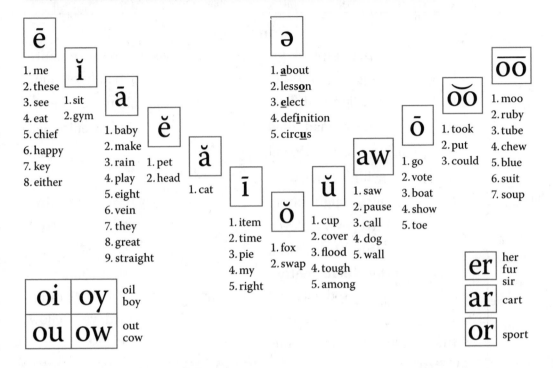

ē
1. me
2. these
3. see
4. eat
5. chief
6. happy
7. key
8. either

ĭ
1. sit
2. gym

ā
1. baby
2. make
3. rain
4. play
5. eight
6. vein
7. they
8. great
9. straight

ĕ
1. pet
2. head

ă
1. cat

ī
1. item
2. time
3. pie
4. my
5. right

ŏ
1. fox
2. swap

ə
1. about
2. lesson
3. elect
4. definition
5. circus

ŭ
1. cup
2. cover
3. flood
4. tough
5. among

aw
1. saw
2. pause
3. call
4. dog
5. wall

ō
1. go
2. vote
3. boat
4. show
5. toe

o͝o
1. took
2. put
3. could

o͞o
1. moo
2. ruby
3. tube
4. chew
5. blue
6. suit
7. soup

| oi | oy | oil
boy |
| ou | ow | out
cow |

| er | her
fur
sir |
| ar | cart |
| or | sport |

Note: The order of spelling examples reflects the relative frequency of incidence for that spelling of the phoneme.

Vowel Chart based on Moats, L.C. (2003). *LETRS: Language Essentials for Teachers of Reading and Spelling*, Module 2 (p. 98). Adapted with permission of the author. All rights reserved. Published by Sopris West Educational Services.

Pronunciation Key

Consonants

p	pup, rapped, pie		zh	vision, treasure, azure
b	bob, ebb, brother		h	hat, here, hope
t	tire, jumped, hurt		ch	church, match, beach
d	deed, mad, filed		j	judge, enjoy, jell
k	cat, kick, cut		m	mop
g	get, gill, magazine		n	not
f	fluff, rough, photo		ng	sing
v	valve, every, eleven		l	land
th	thin, three, math			
th	this, there, mother		w	with, wagon, west
s	sod, city, list		r	ramp
z	zebra, has, bees		y	yard, yes, yellow
sh	ship, sugar, machine			

Vowels

ē	beet	(bēt)		ō	boat	(bōt)
ĭ	bit	(bĭt)		o͝o	put	(po͝ot)
ā	bait	(bāt)		o͞o	boot	(bo͞ot)
ĕ	bet	(bĕt)		oi	boil	(boil)
ă	bat	(băt)		ou	pout	(pout)
ī	bite	(bīt)		î	peer	(pîr)
ŏ	pot	(pŏt)		â	bear	(bâr)
ô	bought	(bôt)		ä	par	(pär)
ŭ	but	(bŭt)		ô	bore	(bôr)
ə	rabbit	(ră′ bət)		û	pearl	(pûrl)

STEP 2

Word Recognition and Spelling

Building Words from Sounds and Letters (Unit 1)

We put vowels and consonants together to make words.

Two words in English are made of just one vowel.

i = I   a = a

All other words combine consonants and vowels.

a + t = at

m + a + t = mat

m + a + s + t = mast

l + a + s + t = last

b + l + a + s + t = blast

Syllables

What is a Syllable? (Unit 3)

Words are made up of parts we call **syllables**.

- Some words have just one syllable.
- Every syllable has one vowel sound.
- A syllable may or may not be a word by itself.

In the word...	How many syllables?		
	1	**2**	**3**
map	map		
bandit	ban	dit	
inhibit	in	hib	it

When a syllable has a vowel followed by at least one **consonant**, the vowel sound (v) is usually short.

ĭt	mă<u>p</u>	bĕ<u>nd</u>
vc	vc	vcc

Syllable Patterns

Note the pattern of vowels (v) and consonants (c).

VC/CV Pattern   (Unit 3)

ban + dit = bandit

vc   cv =   vc/cv

VC/CV Pattern Words			
Unit 3	admit	drastic	mishap	tactic
	attic	fabric	picnic	traffic
	bandit	frantic	plastic	transit
	candid	impact	rabbit	victim
Unit 4	kidnap	napkin	zigzag	
Unit 5	bobbin	coffin	cosmic	mascot
	classic	combat	goblin	nonfat

VC/V Pattern   (Unit 5)

Some two-syllable words have a different pattern.

rob + in = robin

vc   v = vc/v

VC/V Pattern Words			
Unit 5	cabin	limit	rabid	topic
	clinic	livid	rapid	tropic
	comic	manic	robin	valid
	critic	mimic	static	visit
	frolic	panic	timid	vivid
	habit	profit	tonic	
Unit 6	axis	toxic	toxin	

Compound Words

For more about **Compound Words**, see Step 3, page H19.

What is a Compound Word?   (Unit 3)

A **compound word** is made up of two or more smaller words.

In a compound word, both words have to be real words that can stand on their own.

| **sand** | + | **bag** | = | **sandbag** |

Compound Words			
Unit 3	catnip	grandstand	sandbag	
	granddad	handbag	sandblast	
Unit 4	backhand	backtrack	skinflint	
	backpack	pigskin	slapstick	
Unit 5	backdrop	bobcat	hotdog	windmill
	backlog	cannot	jackpot	
	backstop	hilltop	laptop	
Unit 6	hatbox	quicksand	hotbox	sandbox

Spelling Conventions

Spelling tips help us remember conventions about English words. The tips help us spell words.

Words with <u>v</u>   (Unit 3)

This is strange about the letter <u>v</u>: Almost no English words end in <u>v</u>.

At the end of a word, <u>v</u> is almost always followed by <u>e</u>.

> have   give   live

Double Consonants   (Unit 5)

Use double letters **-ss, -ff, -ll, -zz**

- at the end of many words.
- after one short vowel.

> pass   stiff   will   jazz

- in many one-syllable words.

Ways to Spell / *k* /   (Unit 4)

The sound / *k* / is spelled three ways. The position of / *k* / in the word signals how to spell it:

- use <u>c</u> at the beginning of words before the vowel <u>a</u>: <u>c</u>at.
- use <u>k</u> at the beginning of words before the vowel <u>i</u>: <u>k</u>id.
- use **-<u>ck</u>** after one short vowel in one-syllable words: ba<u>ck</u>, si<u>ck</u>.

Spelling Rules

Spelling rules help us add endings to words.

Doubling Rule   (Unit 6)

When a

- 1-syllable word   hop
- with 1 vowel   hop
- ends in 1 consonant   hop

double the final consonant *before* adding a **suffix** that begins with a **vowel**.

This follows the 1-1-1 pattern.

$$\overset{\text{v}}{\text{hop}} + \underset{\text{suffix}}{\underline{\overset{\text{v}}{\text{ing}}}} = \text{hopping}$$

Do not **double** the consonant when the **suffix** begins with a consonant.

$$\text{cap} + \underset{\text{suffix}}{\underline{\overset{\text{c}}{\text{ful}}}} = \text{capful}$$

Write the Base Word	1 - 1 - 1			Suffix	Double?	Write the Base • Suffix
	One Vowel?	One Consonant After the Vowel?	One Syllable?			
1. stop	yes	yes	yes	ing	yes	stopping
2. lock	yes	no	yes	ing	no	locking
3. cap	yes	yes	yes	ful	no	capful

STEP 3

Vocabulary and Morphology

Adding certain letters to words can add to or change their meanings.

Meaning Parts

See also
Noun Forms Step 4, page H26.

Singular Noun   (Unit 1)

Singular means "one of something."

bat = one bat = singular

Adding -s / Plural Noun   (Unit 1)

Adding -s changes a singular noun to a plural noun.

Plural means "more than one."

bats = more than one bat = plural

Adding -s / Singular Present Tense Verb   (Unit 4)

Adding -s signals the number and tense (time) of a verb:

See also
Verb Forms (Tense Timeline), Step 4, page H31.

-s means <u>singular</u> <u>present tense</u>.

one of something   happening now

He **sit**s.

The shovel **dig**s.

The ground **move**s.

Adding -ing / Present Progressive   (Unit 5)

Adding -ing to a verb means an action is ongoing, or in progress.

The -ing ending signals the progressive verb form. Present progressive verbs are preceded by **am**, **are**, or **is**.

I **am** fishing.

The fish **are** swimming.

The sun **is** shining.

Adding 's / Singular Possessive Nouns   (Unit 2)

Adding 's (an apostrophe and an s) to a noun shows ownership, which means possession.

Sam + 's	Rosa + 's	cat + 's
Sam's map	**Rosa's desk**	**cat's paw**
The map belongs to Sam.	The desk belongs to Rosa.	The paw belongs to the cat.

Multiple Meanings   (Unit 1)

Sometimes the same word can mean different things.

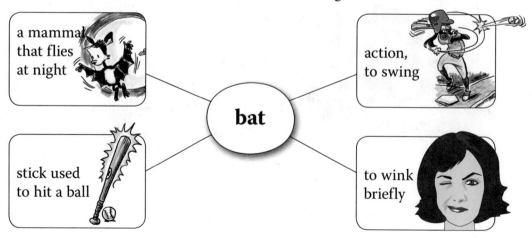

a mammal that flies at night

action, to swing

bat

stick used to hit a ball

to wink briefly

Compound Words

For more about **Compound Words**, see Step 2, page H13.

Understanding the Meaning of Compound Words (Unit 3)

- Often the last part of a compound word provides information about the meaning of the word.

A **sandbag** is a type of **bag**.

- Sometimes the first part and the last part combine to form an entirely new meaning. (Unit 4)

Both **hot** and **dog** are words, but **hotdog** is not a type of dog.

This is a **hot dog**,   but not a **hotdog**.

Idiomatic Expressions (Unit 4)

An idiomatic expression, or **idiom**, is a common phrase that cannot be understood by the meanings of its separate words. The idiom can only be understood by knowing the meaning of the entire phrase. Its words cannot be changed, or the idiom loses its meaning.

Idiom	Meaning	Sample Sentence
hit the sack (Unit 4)	go to bed	I think I will hit the sack early tonight.
be in the swim (Unit 4)	active in the general current of affairs	She is always in the swim of things when it comes to the latest gossip.
be in the wind (Unit 4)	likely to occur; in the offing	There are rumors in the wind about Maria quitting the team.
pat on the back (Unit 4)	congratulate; encourage someone	The coach gave him a pat on the back for the good game.
stick to your ribs (Unit 4)	be substantial or filling (used with food)	Those potatoes will stick to your ribs.
at the drop of a hat (Unit 5)	immediately and without urging	I'll eat ice cream at the drop of a hat.
fit the bill (Unit 5)	be exactly the perfect thing that is needed	That mask will fit the bill for my Halloween costume.
hit the spot (Unit 5)	be exactly right; be refreshing	The cool water hit the spot.
pass the hat (Unit 5)	take up a collection of money	They will pass the hat to help the fire victims.
tilt at windmills (Unit 5)	confront and engage in conflict with an imagined opponent or threat	Her wish never to grow up was to tilt at windmills.

Word Relationships

One way to understand the meaning of a word is to compare it to other words.

Antonyms (Unit 2)

Antonyms have opposite meanings.

Antonyms			
	above	below	
	dead	alive	
	happy	sad	

Synonyms (Unit 3)

Words that have the same or similar meaning are **synonyms**.

Synonyms				
	big	=	large	
	slim	=	thin	
	mad	=	angry	

Attributes (Unit 5)

Words can tell about objects' **attributes**, such as size, parts, color, and function.

Categories and attributes help us define words.

Size
A windmill is **tall**.

Parts
A windmill has a **base and blades**.

Shape
Windmills are **narrow**.

Function
Windmills **catch wind energy to make electric energy**.

Definition
A windmill is a machine with a **base and blades** that **catches wind energy to make electric energy**.

Why? Word History

Letter a—The Anglo-Saxons used the Roman alphabet to write their language. But the Old English language had some sounds (phonemes) that Latin did not have. One of those sounds was the sound we call short / ă /. They used the symbol æ to write the sound. Today, we just use the letter **a**. (Unit 1)

Apostrophe—A long time ago, English people wrote "man's hat" as "mannes hat." The suffix **-es** showed ownership. At that time, people pronounced the **e**. Today we show possession with **'s**. (Unit 2)

Dig—**Dig** probably came into the English language from French in the 1300s. It may be related to the word **ditch**. What do **dig** and **ditch** have in common? Today, people may say they dig something they really like. **Dig** once meant "to study deeply"; if you dug something, you understood it well. (Unit 3)

Twi—The words **twin, two, twenty, twilight, twice**, and **twig** all have something in common. They come from the Old English word **twi**, which meant the number "two." So, a twig divides a branch into two parts. Twins are two persons or things that are similar or identical. (Unit 4)

Jazz—Some say the word **jazz** comes from the name of an African American Chicago musician, Jasbo Brown, who played early jazz. A sports writer, "Scoop" Gleeson, used the word in 1913 to mean active and lively. **Jazz** was first used to refer to a type of music in 1915. (Unit 5)

Toxic and Toxin—The English words **toxic** and **toxin** may come from an Old Persian word *tigra*, which meant *"arrow."* The Greeks changed the word to *toxikon*, which meant "poison for arrows." Later, the Romans borrowed the word from the Greeks. They changed it to *toxicum*, which in Latin meant *"poison."* English borrowed the word from Latin. Today, **toxin** means a poisonous substance. **Toxic** means relating to, or caused by, a harmful substance. (Unit 6)

Grammar and Usage

When we understand words and their meanings, we can use them in sentences. Words have different jobs in sentences. Sometimes the same word can have different jobs depending on how it is used.

Nouns

> Nouns can be singular or plural. See **Meaning Parts** in Step 3, page H16.

What Is a Noun? (Unit 1)

A **noun** names a **person**, a **place**, or a **thing**.

Nouns						
Unit 1	act	cab	cat	fat	mat	tab
	bat	cast	fact	mast	scab	
Unit 2	ant	craft	hat	man	plan	stamp
	cap	fan	jam	map	plant	strap
	camp	flap	lab	pact	raft	tract
	clam	flat	lamp	pan	sap	trap
Unit 3	bag	band	traffic	dig	lip	mint
	flag	gas	dad	land	rib	sand
	picnic	clip	hand	rabbit	van	
	stand	gift	trip	valve	film	

Common and Proper Nouns   (Unit 3)

Nouns may be common or proper.

- A **common noun** names a *general* person, place, or thing.
- A **proper noun** names a *specific* person, place, or thing.

Common Nouns	Proper Nouns
man	Mr. West
city	Boston
statue	Statue of Liberty
land	Badlands
mountain	Pikes Peak

Proper nouns begin with a capital letter.

Concrete and Abstract Nouns   (Unit 3)

Nouns may be concrete or abstract.

- A **concrete noun** names a person, place, or thing that we *can see or touch*.

Concrete Nouns				
table	car	pencil	plate	teacher

- An **abstract noun** names an idea or a thought that we *cannot see or touch*.

Abstract Nouns			
love	Saturday	sports	democracy

Noun Forms

See also
Meaning Parts
Step 3, page H16.

Singular Noun   (Unit 1)

Singular means "one of something."

Plural Noun   (Unit 1)

Adding -**s** changes a singular noun to a plural noun.

Adding the suffix -**s** to a singular noun . . . . makes a plural noun.	
■ map + s = maps	■ I had the **maps** in my bag.
■ cab + s = cabs	■ The **cabs** are fast.
■ mast + s = masts	■ The bats sat on the **masts**.

Singular Possessive Noun   (Unit 2)

Adding **'s** to a noun shows possession.

Adding the suffix **'s** to a singular noun . . . . makes a possessive singular noun.	
■ Stan + 's = Stan's	■ **Stan's** stamps are at camp.
■ van + 's = van's	■ The **van's** mat is flat.
■ man + 's = man's	■ The **man's** cap is black.

Noun Functions

Nouns have several functions (jobs).

Noun as a Subject   (Unit 2)

Nouns can serve as the subjects of sentences.

The **subject**:

- is one of two main parts of English sentences.
- names the person, place, or thing that the sentence is about.
- usually comes before the verb.
- answers "Who (what) did it?"

Ask yourself...

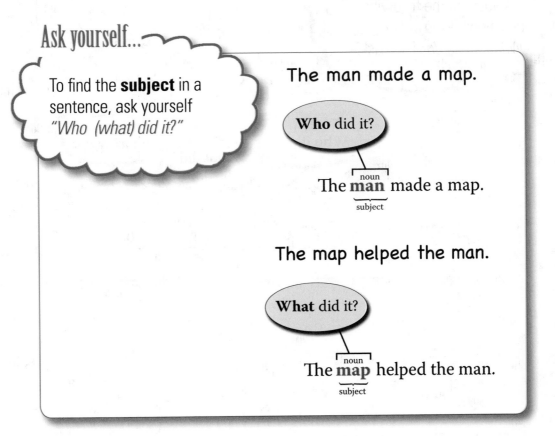

To find the **subject** in a sentence, ask yourself *"Who (what) did it?"*

The man made a map.

Who did it?

noun
The **man** made a map.
subject

The map helped the man.

What did it?

noun
The **map** helped the man.
subject

Noun as a Direct Object (Unit 3)

A noun can be the direct object—the person, place, or thing that receives the action.

The direct object:

- is in the predicate part of the sentence.
- answers "What did they (he, she, it) do it to?"

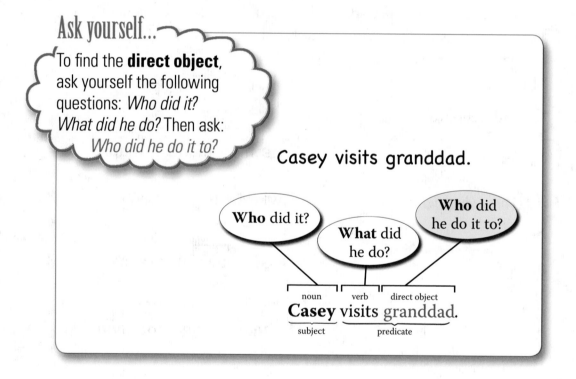

Ask yourself...

To find the **direct object**, ask yourself the following questions: *Who did it? What did he do?* Then ask: *Who did he do it to?*

Casey visits granddad.

Who did it?

What did he do?

Who did he do it to?

| noun | verb | direct object |

Casey visits granddad.

subject · predicate

Noun as an Object of the Preposition   (Unit 4)

A noun can be the **object of the preposition** in a prepositional phrase.

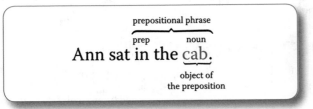

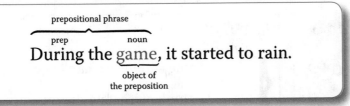

Verbs

Verbs describe actions. **(Unit 1)**

We **can see** some actions:

jump, walk, and clap

Some actions we **can't see**:

think, wish, and dream

Verbs						
Unit 1	act	bat	cast	sat		
Unit 2	blast	flap	clap	trap	scan	plant
	clamp	strap	slam	ran	nap	
	fan	tramp	snap	rap	plan	
	rant	map	stamp	scrap	ram	
	pant	can	tap	slap	span	
Unit 4	ask	risk	track	zip	pack	
	swim	zap	skip	pick	sack	
	win	kick	skid	crack	twist	
Unit 5	bill	stop	spill	rob	jog	drill
	rock	sniff	lock	nod	mob	fill
	cross	spot	mock	golf	drop	grill
	block	wilt	prompt	hop	dock	clog

Verb Forms

Verbs describe action. Verbs also signal time. **(Unit 4)**

Tense Timeline **(Unit 4)**

A **tense timeline** shows three points in time—past, present, and future.

Yesterday	Today	Tomorrow
Past	Present	Future

Present Tense **(Unit 4)**

If something is happening right now, it is the present tense.

For third person singular, add **-s** to the verb to signal present tense.

Person	Singular	Plural
First Person	I sit.	We sit.
Second Person	You sit.	You sit.
Third Person	He (She, It) sits.	They sit.

Yesterday	Today	Tomorrow
Past	Present	Future
	-s	
	He bats.	
	She jogs.	
	It sits.	

The Verb *Be* (Unit 5)

- **Am**, **is**, and **are** are all present tense forms of the verb **be**.

- Forms of **be** can be used as helping verbs.

- Different forms of **be** are used with different personal pronouns to achieve subject-verb agreement in sentences.

Correct Use of Present Tense Forms of *Be*		
Person	**Singular**	**Plural**
First Person	I **am** packing	We **are** packing.
Second Person	You **are** packing.	You **are** packing.
Third Person	He (She, It) **is** packing.	They **are** packing.

Present Progressive (Unit 5)

Add -**ing** to the verb and use the helping verb **am**, **is**, or **are** in front of the verb to make the present progressive.

Person	**Singular**	**Plural**
First Person	I am sitting.	We are sitting.
Second Person	You are sitting.	You are sitting.
Third Person	He (She, It) is sitting.	They are sitting.

Verb Functions

Predicate   (Unit 2)

The **predicate** is the second of the two main parts of a sentence.

The **predicate:**

- contains the main verb of the sentence.
- describes the action.
- usually comes after the subject.
- answers "What did they (he, she, it) do?"

Ask yourself...

To find the **predicate**, ask yourself the following question: Who did it? Then ask: *What did he do?*

The man ran.

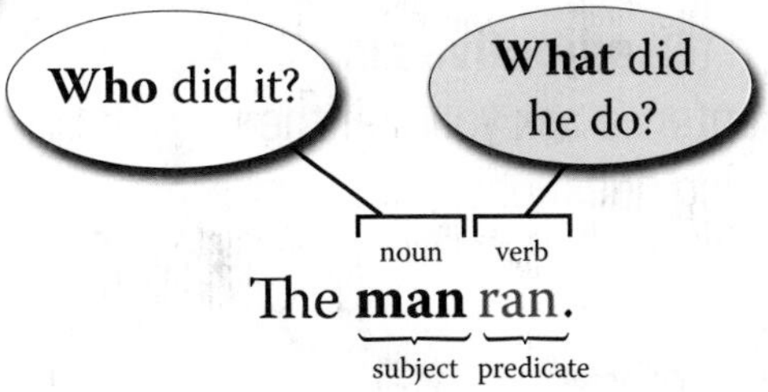

Who did it?

What did he do?

noun   verb

The **man** ran.

subject   predicate

Adjectives describe nouns.

They answer:

- *how many?*
- *what kind?*
- *which one?*

Some prepositional phrases act like adjectives because they can also tell about attributes of a noun. These phrases begin with a preposition and end with a noun.

The subject of the sentence can have adjectives and prepositional phrases that act as adjectives describing the person, place, or thing that the sentence is about.

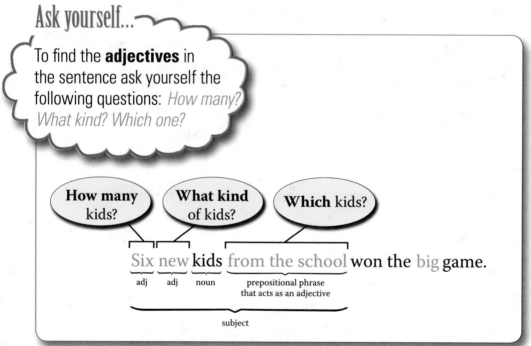

Ask yourself...

To find the **adjectives** in the sentence ask yourself the following questions: *How many? What kind? Which one?*

How many kids?   **What kind** of kids?   **Which** kids?

Six new **kids** from the school won the big game.

adj   adj   noun   prepositional phrase that acts as an adjective

subject

Adjectives can also describe other nouns in the sentence.

What kind of game? big

Adverbs (Unit 6)

For more about **Prepositions**, see Step 4, page H36.

Adverbs are words that describe verbs.

Adverbs and prepositional phrases that act as adverbs tell:

- *when?*
- *where?*
- *how?*

Some prepositional phrases act like adverbs. Prepositional phrases begin with a preposition and end with a noun. **On Monday, in the house, with a bang,** and **to the class** are prepositional phrases.

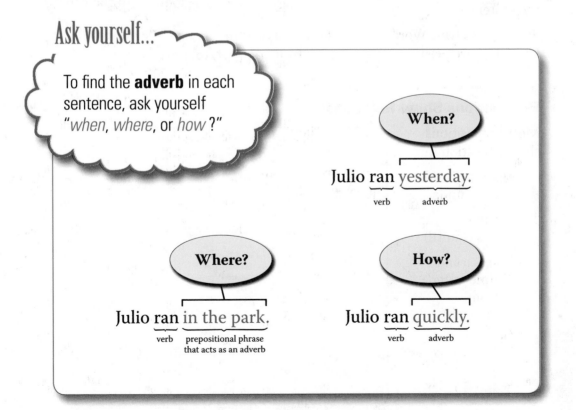

Ask yourself...

To find the **adverb** in each sentence, ask yourself "*when*, *where*, or *how*?"

When?

Julio ran yesterday.
verb   adverb

Where?

Julio ran in the park.
verb   prepositional phrase
        that acts as an adverb

How?

Julio ran quickly.
verb   adverb

A **preposition** is a function word that begins a prepositional phrase.

A **prepositional phrase** is a group of words that begins with a preposition and ends with a noun or pronoun that is the **object of the preposition**.

Prepositions show the position or relationship between the noun or pronoun and some other word in the sentence.

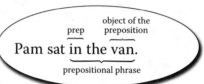

In this sentence, **in** (the preposition) shows a relationship between **van** (the object of the preposition) and **Pam** (the subject of the sentence).

Some of the Unit Words and Essentials Words in Units 1–4 are prepositions: in, as, at, from, of, past, to, into.

Prepositions Show Relationship   (Unit 6)

Most prepositions show a position in

- space (inside, over, under)

- time (during, since, until)

- space and time (after, from, through)

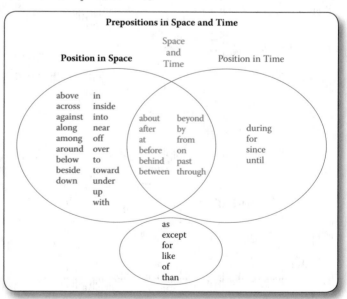

Pronouns (Unit 4)

Pronouns are function words that are used in place of nouns.
Different groups of pronouns have different functions.

Subject (Nominative) Pronouns (Unit 4)

Nominative pronouns take the place of the subject in a sentence.

I, you, he, she, it, we, you, and **they** are nominative pronouns.

Jack sat in a cab.

He sat in a **cab**.

(**He** replaces **Jack** in the sentence.)

Subject Pronouns		
Person	**Singular**	**Plural**
First Person	I	we
Second Person	you	you
Third Person	he, she, it	they

Object Pronouns   (Unit 6)

Some pronouns take the place of **objects**. They are called **object pronouns**.

Me, **you**, **him**, **her**, **it**, **us**, and **them** are object pronouns.

Carla is handing the plant to **Sally**.
Carla is handing the plant to **her**.

(**Her** replaces Sally in the sentence.)

Object Pronouns		
Person	**Singular**	**Plural**
First Person	me	us
Second Person	you	you
Third Person	him, her, it	them

Multiple Functions of Words

In English, words have different functions (jobs). **(Unit 3)**

Nouns are words that name people, places, or things.

Verbs are words that describe action.

Adjectives describe nouns. **(Unit 6)**

Sometimes the same word can have multiple functions.
The context helps determine the function of the word.

For example, the word **dig** can be a noun or a verb.

Dig can also be an adjective. **(Unit 6)**

Noun:

The **dig** was a success in Africa.

Verb:

Scientists **dig** to find bones.

Adjective:

The scientists went to the **dig** site.

What is a Sentence?   (Unit 1)

Sentences convey a complete thought by answering two questions:

❶ Who (What) did it?

❷ What did they (he, she, it) do?

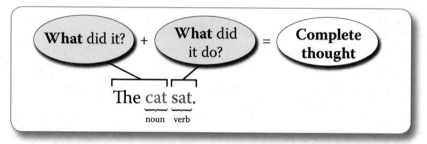

We put nouns and verbs together to make **sentences**.

Simple Sentences   (Unit 2)

A **simple sentence** has one subject and one predicate.

- The subject answers: "Who (What) did it?"
- The verb in the predicate answers: "What did they (he, she, it) do?"

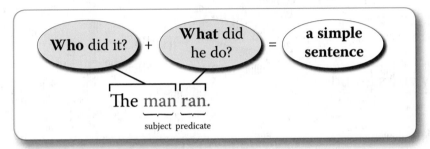

Diagram It!—Simple Sentence

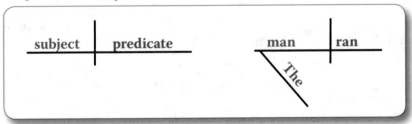

Sentence Expansion

For more about **Noun as a Direct Object**, see Step 4, page H28.

Predicate Expansion with Direct Object   (Unit 3)

You can expand the predicate in a sentence by adding a direct object.

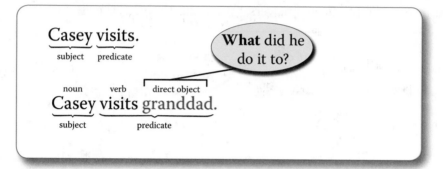

Diagram It!—Direct Object

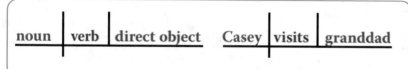

Predicate Expansion with Adverbs   (Unit 4)

You can expand the predicate in a sentence by adding
adverbs or prepositional phrases that act like adverbs.

See also
Writing Sentences,
Step 6, page H56.
See **Adverbs,**
page H35.

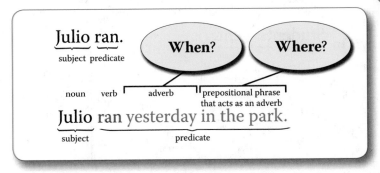

Moving Adverbs in a Sentence   (Unit 5)

Words or phrases that answer the questions "when, where, or how"
can be moved within the sentence.

Diagram It!—Adverbs

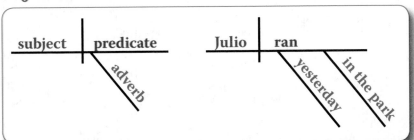

Subject Expansion with Adjectives (Unit 6)

You can expand the subject of a sentence by adding adjectives.

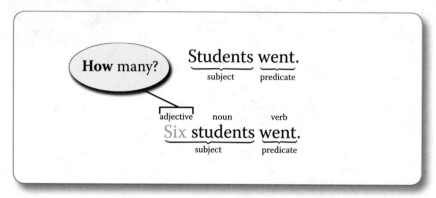

Diagram It!—Adjectives

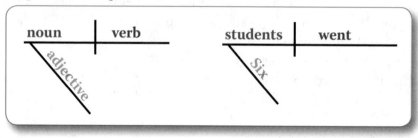

Mechanics   (Unit 5)

Phrases with Commas

Commas are used to signal a pause when reading or writing to clarify meaning.

Commas can be used to set off phrases at the beginning of sentences.

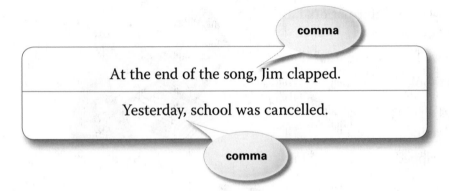

At the end of the song, Jim clapped.

Yesterday, school was cancelled.

Sentence Signals   (Unit 1)

Capital letters are used at the **beginning** of all sentences.

Punctuation marks are used at the **ending** of all sentences.

Periods, question marks, and exclamation points can be used to end a sentence.

The cat sat.   Where did it sit?   It sat on my lap!

STEP 5

Listening and Reading Comprehension

Types of Text

There are two main categories of text: **expository** and **narrative**.

Expository text is informational. It is also called nonfiction.

Where do we find informational text?

- Textbooks
- Newspapers
- Magazines
- Encyclopedias

Narrative text tells a story.

Where do we find narratives?

- Novels
- Anthologies
- Magazines
- Comic books

👂 Listening Tips

Demonstrate active listening by:

- Asking questions for clarification and understanding
- Comparing what is heard to prior knowledge and experiences
- Identifying fact and opinion in visual media

Create a map or informal outline while listening

Determine the purpose for listening (e.g., enjoyment, information, etc.)

Text Features (Unit 1)

Writers of **informational text**—also called **nonfiction**—use **text features** to provide clues to the topic and other important information.

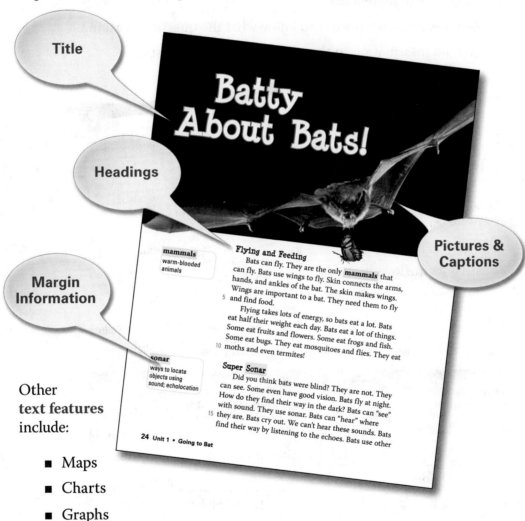

Title

Headings

Pictures & Captions

Margin Information

Batty About Bats!

mammals
warm-blooded animals

Flying and Feeding

Bats can fly. They are the only **mammals** that can fly. Bats use wings to fly. Skin connects the arms, hands, and ankles of the bat. The skin makes wings. Wings are important to a bat. They need them to fly
5 and find food.

Flying takes lots of energy, so bats eat a lot. Bats eat half their weight each day. Bats eat a lot of things. Some eat fruits and flowers. Some eat frogs and fish. Some eat bugs. They eat mosquitoes and flies. They eat
10 moths and even termites!

sonar
ways to locate objects using sound; echolocation

Super Sonar

Did you think bats were blind? They are not. They can see. Some even have good vision. Bats fly at night. How do they find their way in the dark? Bats can "see" with sound. They use sonar. Bats can "hear" where
15 they are. Bats cry out. We can't hear these sounds. Bats find their way by listening to the echoes. Bats use other

24 Unit 1 • Going to Bat

Other **text features** include:

- Maps
- Charts
- Graphs

For more about **Writing Sentences,** see Step 6, page H56.

Comprehension Questions

How to answer open-ended questions (Unit 1)

Use these steps to answer a short-answer question with a complete sentence:

❶ Look for a signal word to know what the question is asking.

❷ Find information in the text to answer the question.

❸ Plan and write the answer.

❹ Check the answer.

Example question:

Are all bats bug-eaters?

Look for the signal word

No, some bats eat fruits or flowers.

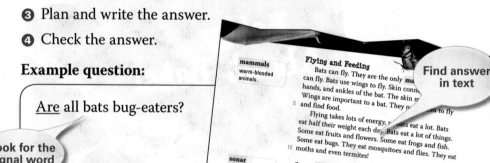

Find answer in text

Flying and Feeding
Bats can fly. They are the only ma___ can fly. Bats use wings to fly. Skin conn___ hands, and ankles of the bat. The skin m___ Wings are important to a bat. They n___ ___m to fly
5   and find food.
Flying takes lots of energy, s___ ___ats eat a lot. Bats eat half their weight each da___. Bats eat a lot of things. Some eat fruits and flowers. Some eat frogs and fish. Some eat bugs. They eat mosquitoes and flies. They eat
10 moths and even termites!

mammals
warm-blooded animals

sonar
ways to locate objects using sound; echolocation

Super Sonar
Did you think bats were blind? They are not. They can see. Some even have good vision. Bats fly at night. How do they find their way in the dark? Bats can "see" with sound. They use sonar. Bats can "hear" where
15 they are. Bats cry out. We can't hear these sounds. Bats find their way by listening to the echoes. Bats use other

24 Unit 1 • Going to Bat

Signal words help you know how to answer the question.

Signal words	How to answer
If the question asks...	**Your answer must include...**
Is/are	A "yes" or a "no"
Who	Information about a person or group
Do/does	A "yes" or a "no"
What	An action or name of a thing
When	A specific time, date, or event
Why	A reason or explanation
Where	A general location or specific place
How	The way something is done

How to answer multiple-choice questions   (Unit 3)

Use these steps to answer multiple-choice questions:

❶ Read carefully for signal words.

❷ Look back in the text for information.

❸ Try to eliminate distracter items.

Example question:

The Touareg are

(A) a tribe of people who live in Niger.

(B) special dinosaurs in Africa.

(C) big animals that live in Africa.

(D) scientists who work in Niger.

Africa Digs

Dr. Paul Sereno digs dinosaur bones. He gets a thrill when he digs up the bones of dinosaurs who lived thousands of years ago. In 1997, Dr. Sereno led a dig to **Niger**, Africa. He took 18 scientists with him.
5 The Touareg tribe helped his team look for bones. The Touareg people live in Niger. They know their **desert** land best. They know where to look for bones.

The dig was a success. Dr. Sereno's team had a fantastic find. They found a new dinosaur. The
10 Touareg told them a legend about a very big animal. They call it *Jobar*. The Touareg showed them where to look for the bones. The scientists named the dinosaur *Jobaria*. It means giant. How did they dig up the *Jobaria*? Let's follow the dig step by step.

Step 1: We've Got One!
15   The Touareg lead the team to a special place. Bones stick out of desert rock. The Touareg tell the scientists their legend. These bones belong to the giant beast, *Jobar*.

Step 2: Digging In
20   The dig begins. They use hammers, chisels, and drills. They work for 10 weeks. A huge skeleton **emerges**. It has been buried for 135 million years! Fifteen tons of rock cover it. The team carefully
25 takes the bones from the rock.

Niger
a country of west Africa

desert
a dry place with little rainfall

emerges
comes out of; appears

80 Unit 3 • Dig It!

The Touareg tribe helped the team.

Structure of Text   (Unit 1)

Well-written text has organization. Informational text is organized using main ideas and supporting details.

The main idea tells what the paragraph is about.
The supporting details give more specific information about the main idea.

Ask yourself...
Which sentence tells what all of the sentences are about?

Ask yourself...
Which sentences support the main idea?

The bat can fly. It is the only mammal that can fly. Bats use wings to fly. Skin connects parts of the bat. It joins its hands, arms, and ankles. The skin makes wings. Bats fly to look for food. They fly at night. They need their wings to eat. Bats eat a lot. Bats eat half their weight each day! Food makes energy. Flying takes energy. Bats eat a lot of things. Some eat fruits. Some eat flowers. Some eat frogs and fish. Some eat lizards. Some eat bugs. They eat mosquitoes. They eat flies. They eat moths. They even eat termites!

STEP 6 Speaking and Writing

Structure of Writing (Unit 1)

Graphic organizers can show the structure of text. The **Blueprint for Writing** is a graphic organizer that shows the relationship between the main ideas (walls) and supporting details (pictures on the walls).

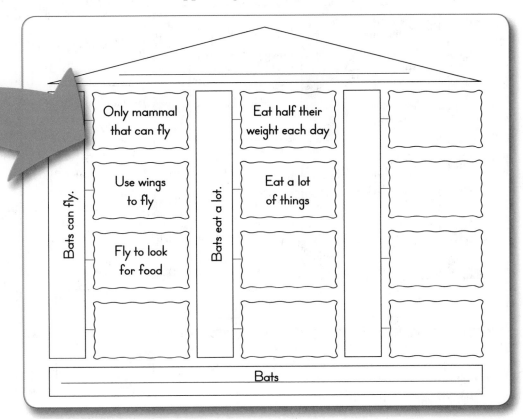

Simple Summary   (Unit 1)

A summary tells the most important ideas from a text selection.
A **simple summary** uses only the main ideas (walls).

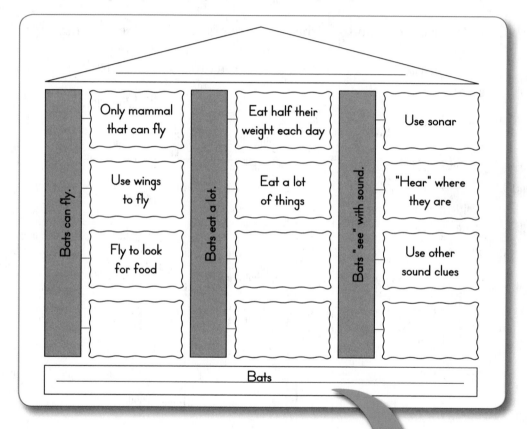

Bats can fly.	Bats eat a lot.	Bats "see" with sound.
Only mammal that can fly	Eat half their weight each day	Use sonar
Use wings to fly	Eat a lot of things	"Hear" where they are
Fly to look for food		Use other sound clues

Bats

"Batty About Bats!" explains facts about bats. Bats can fly. They eat a lot. Bats "see" with sound.

Expanded Summary   (Unit 1)

Sometimes a summary has more detail. An **expanded summary** uses main ideas (walls) and some supporting details (pictures).

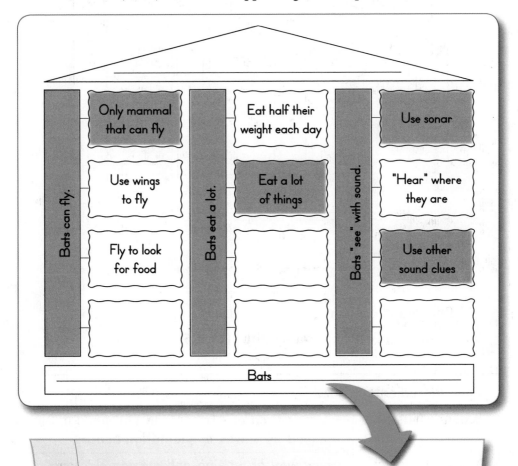

Graphic organizers and outlines help organize information to plan to write.

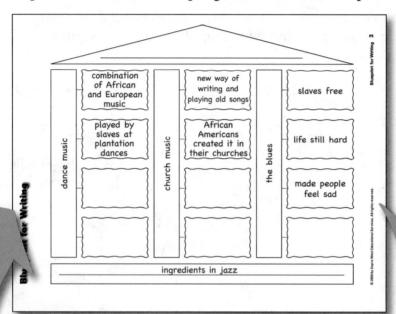

Both graphic organizers can organize the same information.

Informal (Two-Column) Outline (Unit 5)

Topic: ingredients in jazz

☆ dance music	—combination of African and European music —played by slaves at plantation dances
☆ church music	—new way of writing and playing old songs —African Americans created it in their churches
☆ the blues	—slaves free —life still hard —made people feel sad

Speaking Tips

- Speak clearly and at an appropriate pace
- Make eye contact with listeners
- Stay on topic
- Organize content in a logical sequence
- Use specific vocabulary

Sentences are pictures in words. To write a **Masterpiece Sentence** follow these steps.

Stage 1: Prepare Your Canvas (Unit 1)

Write the base sentence. Answer these questions.

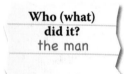

Who (what) did it?	What did they (he, she, it) do?
the man	ran

Stage 2: Paint Your Predicate (Unit 3)

Expand the predicate. Use these questions.

When?	Where?	How?
during the race	on the track	fast

the **man ran** fast on the track during the race

Stage 3: Move the Predicate Painters (Unit 5)

Vary the sentence. Move the predicate painters. Notice the picture *doesn't* change!

during the race the **man ran** fast on the track

Stage 4: Paint Your Subject   (Unit 6)

Expand the subject. Use these questions.

How many?	Which are?	What kind?
	in the red shirt	

during the race the **man** in the red
shirt **ran** fast on the track

Stage 5: Paint Your Words

Improve your words. Be descriptive.

During the race the **man** in the
red shirt ran fast on the track.

During the last lap of the race the
track star wearing his team's red
shirt **sprinted** around the track as fans cheered.

Stage 6: Finishing Touches

Check spelling and punctuation.

> During the last lap of the race, the track star,
> wearing his team's red shirt, sprinted around the
> track as fans cheered.

Writing Paragraphs

Parts of a Paragraph

A paragraph is a group of sentences. Each sentence in the paragraph has a specific job.

The Benefits of Exercise

Regular exercise benefits people's health in two important ways. (One) benefit is that exercise improves people's physical health. It makes the heart, lungs, bones, and muscles stronger and keeps people at a healthy weight. Exercise is (also) good for the mind. It makes people feel better about themselves and calms them down when they are angry or stressed. When people regularly do physical activities they enjoy, their bodies and minds stay fit, happy, and healthy.

The **Topic Sentence** tells what the paragraph is about.

Supporting Details give facts or reasons about the topic.

(Transition words) link one supporting detail to the next.

E's add interest for the reader. E's are:
- **explanations**
- **examples**
- **evidence**

The **conclusion** ties the parts together. Often it restates the topic.

Topic Sentence

The **topic sentence** in a paragraph states the topic of the paragraph. It is often the first sentence.

There are many types of topic sentences. Here are three of them.

IVF Topic Sentence   (Unit 1)

An **IVF topic sentence** has three parts. It is a good type of topic sentence for a summary paragraph.

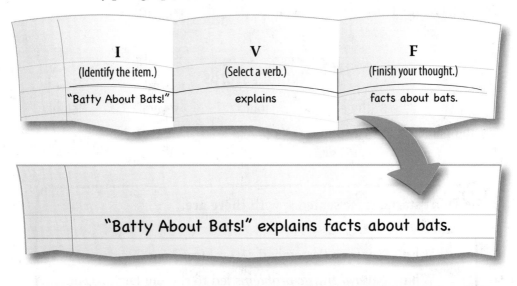

I	V	F
(Identify the item.)	(Select a verb.)	(Finish your thought.)
"Batty About Bats!"	explains	facts about bats.

"Batty About Bats!" explains facts about bats.

Verb Reference List for Summaries

explains	compares	tells	provides	presents
describes	gives	shows	lists	teaches

Number Topic Sentence (Unit 3)

A **Number topic sentence** includes the topic and a number word. The `topic` tells what the whole paragraph will be about. The **number** tells how many supporting details to include about the topic.

Three `problems led to the Big Dig project in Boston`.

Boston leaders identified **several** `traffic problems`.

> ## Number Words
>
> | two | three | four | several | some |
> |---|---|---|---|---|
> | a number of | a few | a couple | many | |

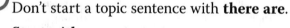

> Don't start a topic sentence with **there are**.
>
> **Start with:**
>
> **Who**: *People in Boston* had several traffic problems.
>
> **What**: *Several traffic problems* led to the Big Dig project.
>
> **When**: *After years of traffic troubles*, three issues led to the Big Dig project.
>
> **Where**: *In Boston*, a number of traffic problems led to the Big Dig.

Turn Prompt Topic Sentence   (Unit 4)

A **Turn Prompt topic sentence** works well to answer a specific question. Part of the prompt becomes part of the topic sentence. Direction words, such as **explains**, tell you what you need to do.

> **Prompt:**
>
> Write a paragraph that <u>explains</u> how maps are made.
>
> **Topic sentence:**
>
> Maps are made in several layers.

Supporting Details

Supporting Details (Unit 3)

Supporting details are sentences that provide **facts** or **reasons** to support a topic sentence.

Transition words link supporting details within a paragraph.

Transition Sets		
First of all ▶	The next ▶	Another
One ▶	Also	
One ▶	Another ▶	Finally
One example ▶	Another example	
The first ▶	The second ▶	Last

Find the supporting details and transition words in "The Benefits of Exercise" on page H58.

E's Are Elaborations

The E's   (Unit 5)

The E's are sentences that support the topic and supporting details in a paragraph.

Here are three kinds of E's. There are more!

*E*xamples give <u>illustrations</u>.

> With a punch of a button, we can download a favorite song to a mini computer.

*E*xplanations give <u>additional information</u>.

> We can get almost any music we want from the World Wide Web.

*E*vidence is data or facts that prove <u>something is true</u>.

> In 2006, one company said it sold three million music downloads a day!

Find these E's in "Computer Music" on the next page. Look for the supporting details on which they elaborate.

Conclusion

Concluding Sentence   (Unit 5)

The concluding sentence in a paragraph often restates the topic sentence.

Computer Music

Computers are changing the way we make and listen to music. For one thing, the computer has changed how we create songs. For example, composers can write concert music on laptops. Musicians can even make their computers "sing" like a huge choir. And DJs can use computer "drum machines" to lay down beats for their next hip hop show. Computers are also changing the way we listen to tunes. We can get almost any music we want from the World Wide Web. With a punch of a button, we can download a favorite song to a mini computer. These mini computers are called MP3 players. They let us take music almost anywhere. In 2006, one company said it sold three million music downloads a day! According to a computer magazine, the number of downloads will keep growing. New technology offers new ways to make and hear beautiful music.

Topic Sentence

Conclusion

Six Traits of Effective Writing (Unit 2)

Trait	What does this mean?
Ideas and Content	Focus on the main ideas or story line. Supporting details (expository) or images/events (narrative) build understanding.
Organization	Order of ideas and supporting details (expository) or clear beginning, middle, and end (narrative) make sense. Introduction, transitions, and conclusion help keep the reader hooked on the writing.
Voice and Audience Awareness	Style suits both the audience and purpose of the writing.
Word Choice	"Just right" words for the topic and audience.
Sentence Fluency	Varied sentence use; no run-on sentences and sentence fragments.
Conventions	Spelling, punctuation, grammar and usage, capitalization, and indenting paragraphs.

Editor's Marks

∧ add or change text
ꝗ delete text
∽ move text
¶ new paragraph
≡ capitalize
/ lowercase
⊙ insert period
◯ check spelling or spell out word

Writer's Checklist for Book A   (Unit 2)

Trait	Did I...?	Unit
Ideas and Content	❑ Focus all sentences on the topic	1
	❑ Provide supporting details for my topic sentence	1
	❑ Include examples, evidence, and/or explanations to develop the supporting detail sentences	5
Organization	❑ Write a topic sentence	1
	❑ Tell things in an order that makes sense	1
	❑ Use transition words and/or phrases	4
	❑ Write a concluding sentence	5
Voice and Audience Awareness	❑ Think about my audience and purpose for writing	6
	❑ Write in a clear and engaging way that makes my audience want to read my work; can my reader "hear" me speaking	6
Word Choice	❑ Try to find my own way to say things	2
	❑ Use words that are lively and specific to the content	2
Sentence Fluency	❑ Write complete sentences	1
	❑ Expand some of my sentences by painting the subject and/or predicate	3, 6
Conventions	Capitalize words correctly:	
	❑ Capitalize the first word of each sentence	1
	❑ Capitalize proper nouns, including people's names	3
	Punctuate correctly:	
	❑ Put a period or question mark at the end of each sentence	1
	❑ Put an apostrophe before the **s** for a singular possessive noun	2
	❑ Use a comma after a long adverb phrase at the beginning of a sentence	5
	Use grammar correctly:	
	❑ Use the correct verb tense	4
	❑ Make sure the verb agrees with the subject in number	4
	Spell correctly:	
	❑ Spell all **Essential Words** correctly	1
	Apply spelling rules	
	❑ The doubling rule (1-1-1)	6

Draft Paragraph

Editor's Marks

∧	add or change text
ℓ	delete text
○→	move text
¶	new paragraph
≡	capitalize
/	lowercase
⊙	insert period
○	check spelling or spell out word

Let's Work Out!

Regular exercise helps people in two important ways It improves people's health. It make the hart, lungs, bones, and muscles stronger. Workin' out is also good for the mind. It makes people feel better about themselves. It calms them down when they feel bad. People should get exercise.

Draft Paragraph with Edits

The Benefits of Exercise ∧ **Let's Work Out!** ℓ

Regular exercise helps people in two

First,
important ways. It improves people's health.

S
It make the ~~hart~~ lungs, bones, and muscles
∧

It keeps people at a healthy weight. Exercise
stronger. Workin~~ out~~ is also good for the mind.
∧

It makes people feel better about themselves.

angry or stressed
It calms them down when they feel ~~bad~~.
∧   ∧

~~People should get exercise.~~

When people get exercise, they stay fit, healthy, and happy.

Revised Paragraph

The Benefits of Exercise

Regular exercise helps people in two important ways. First, it improves people's health. It makes the heart, lungs, bones, and muscles stronger. It keeps people at a healthy weight. Exercise is also good for the mind. It makes people feel better about themselves. It calms them down when they feel angry or stressed. When people get exercise, they stay fit, healthy, and happy.

Ideas and Content: added another explanation

Organization: added a transition

Voice: used a more formal tone of voice for a school paper

Word Choice: used more specific words

Sentence Fluency: wrote a longer sentence

Conventions: corrected spelling, punctuation, and grammar errors

Word List

Essential Words

a, are, I, is, that, the, this

Unit Words

act	bat	fast
am	cat	fat
at	fact	sat

Spelling Lists

Lessons 1–5

a	sat
are	tab
fat	that
I	the
is	this

Lessons 6–10

act	cab
am	cat
as	fact
at	fast
bat	tact

Word List

Essential Words

do, said, to, who, you, your

Unit Words

abstract	clap	jam	past	slam
an	fan	lamp	pat	slap
ant	flap	last	plan	strap
as	flat	man	plant	tan
blast	ham	map	ran	tap
can	has	nap	rat	trap
cap	hat	pan	sap	

Spelling Lists

Lessons 1–5

can	said
do	to
has	who
man	you
map	your

Lessons 6–10

an	lamp
asp	last
cap	plant
clap	raft
flat	strap

Word List

Essential Words

from, of, they, was, were, what

Unit Words

add	damp	give	hit	mad	sand
and	did	glad	if	mint	sin
bad	dig	grab	in	mitt	sip
bag	dim	grant	inn	picnic	sit
band	draft	grin	intrinsic	pig	slim
bib	drag	grip	is	pin	stand
big	fig	had	it	pit	tag
bit	film	hand	land	print	tin
clip	fit	have	lift	rabbit	traffic
crisp	flag	hid	lip	rib	transit
dad	gas	him	list	rip	transmit
dam	gift	his	live	sad	trip

Spelling Lists

Lessons 1–5

did	they
dig	van
from	was
gas	were
of	what

Lessons 6–10

add	handbag
clip	have
damp	list
film	picnic
give	rabbit

Word List

Essential Words

be, does, he, she, we, when

Unit Words

ask	lick	skin	track
back	mask	skip	trick
black	milk	snack	twig
brick	pack	stack	twin
jack	pick	stick	twist
kick	sack	swift	win
kid	sick	swim	wind
kit	silk	task	

Spelling Lists

Lessons 1–5

ask	kick
be	she
black	twin
does	we
he	when

Lessons 6–10

backpack	sick
mask	skip
milk	swim
napkin	wind
pack	zigzag

Word List

Essential Words

here, there, these, those, where, why

Unit Words

bill	dock	gill	kill	odd	sniff
block	dog	glass	kiss	off	sock
blond	doll	golf	lock	on	soft
blot	dot	got	log	pass	spill
bond	drill	grass	lost	pill	spot
boss	drop	grill	lot	pop	stiff
cannot	fill	hill	mill	pot	still
class	fizz	hop	miss	rob	stock
clock	flock	hot	mob	rock	stop
cost	font	ill	mop	rot	top
crop	frog	jazz	nod	sill	will
cross	frost	job	not	smog	

Spelling Lists

Lessons 1–5

cross	those
here	top
lock	where
there	why
these	will

Lessons 6–10

boss	jazz
cabin	off
cannot	profit
classic	rock
critic	visit

Word List

Essential Words

down, for, her, how, me, now

Unit Words

box	quack	tax
fix	quick	toxic
fox	quilt	toxins
mix	six	wax

Spelling Lists

Lessons 1–5

down	me
for	now
fox	quack
her	quick
how	six

Lessons 6–10

axis	quitting
fix	sandbox
quicksand	toxic
quilt	toxins
quints	wax

Bonus Words

Unit 1

ab	cast	scab	stab
bam	mast	scam	tab
cab	mat	scat	tact

Unit 2

aft	camp	lab	ramp	snap
alp	clam	lap	rant	span
amp	clamp	nab	rap	spat
asp	clasp	pact	scan	stamp
ban	crab	pal	scrap	stat
blab	craft	pant	slab	tract
bran	cram	raft	slant	tramp
brat	flab	ram	slat	

Unit 3

ad	candid	fad	glib	handbag
admit	catnip	fib	glint	hint
attic	classic	fin	graft	hip
bandit	crib	fist	gram	imp
bid	din	flint	grand	impact
bin	dip	flip	granddad	jag
bland	drab	flit	grandstand	jilt
blip	drastic	frantic	grasp	lag
brag	drift	gab	grid	lid
brand	drip	gap	grim	limp
brim	fabric	gland	grit	lint

Unit 3 continued

lisp	plastic	sandblast	spin	tip
lit	prim	script	sprint	trig
mantis	primp	sift	stilt	trim
misfit	rag	silt	strand	valve
mishap	rid	slid	strict	van
mist	rift	slip	strip	vast
nag	rig	slit	tactic	vat
nip	rim	snag	tidbit	victim
pad	sag	snip	tilt	
pip	sandbag	snit	tint	

Unit 4

backhand	disk	rack	slapstick	wisp
backpack	flick	risk	slick	wit
backtrack	frisk	skid	smack	yak
bask	kidnap	skim	tack	yam
blitz	kin	skim milk	tick	yap
brisk	lack	skimp	wag	zap
clack	napkin	skinflint	wick	zigzag
click	nick	skit	wig	zip
crack	pigskin	slack	wilt	

Bonus Words

Unit 5

ascot	cop	handbill	mom	slot
backdrop	cosmic	hilltop	moss	smock
backlog	cot	hiss	nonfat	snob
backstop	crisscross	hock	opt	sob
bass	critic	hog	panic	sod
bliss	dill	hotdog	plod	staff
bobbin	dog tag	inhibit	plop	static
bobcat	don	jackpot	plot	stockings
brass	flop	jock	pod	stomp
cabin	floss	jog	pond	till
cliff	fog	jot	prod	timid
clinic	fond	lapdog	profit	tonic
clog	frill	limit	prom	topic
clot	frizz	livid	prompt	toss
cob	frock	lob	prop	trill
cod	frolic	loft	rabid	trod
coffin	frond	loss	rapid	tropic
cog	glob	manic	robin	trot
combat	gloss	mascot	rod	valid
comic	goblin	mimic	romp	visit
comic strip	gobs	mock	skill	vivid
con	habit	mod	slop	windmill

Unit 6

ax	hatbox	pox	quints	sandbox
axis	hotbox	quicksand	quip	sax
fax	lax	quid	quit	sox
flax	nix	quill	quiz	toxin

Text Selections

"*What we play is life.*"
– Louis Armstrong (1900-1971)

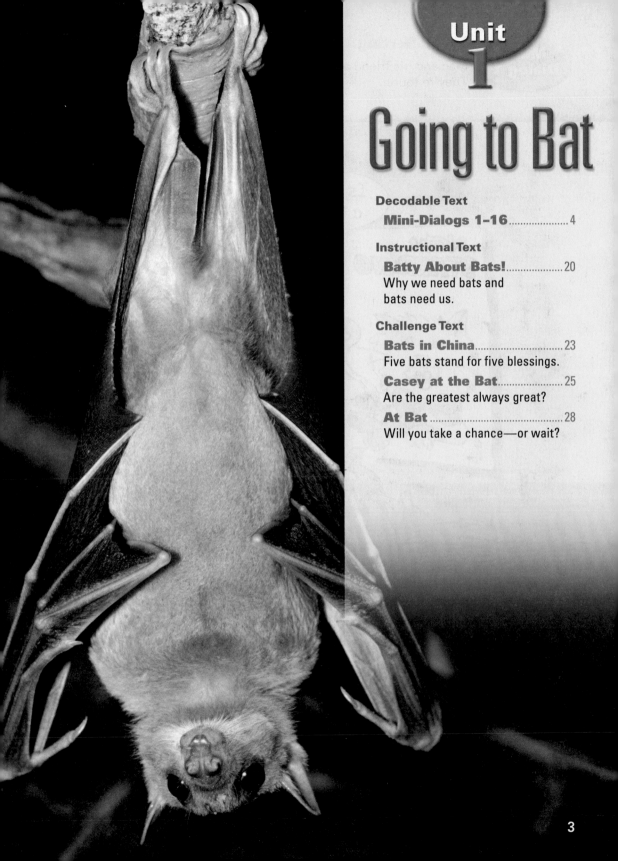

Unit 1

Going to Bat

Stage Setting

Mac and his friend are alley cats. They live on the streets. They're tough.

Critic's Corner

1. What do Mac and his friend think of Samantha (Sam), the actress?

2. Why would Mac say that Sam is "**not** a cat"?

Mini-Dialog 2

Stage Setting

It's late at night. Bats are out, flying and feeding. The theater has just closed.

Critic's Corner

1. What do the bats think of Sam?

2. What does Sam think of the bats?

Critic's Corner

1. The painting is abstract. What do you think the term *abstract art* means?

2. Do you think these people really like the painting?

Mini-Dialog 4

Stage Setting
In the art gallery, we can learn as much about people as we can about art.

Critic's Corner

1. Abstract art can be just line and color, a picture of an idea. People want to see a thing. Why do people search for a thing in paintings?

2. Do these two people really enjoy the art?

Mini-Dialog 5

Stage Setting

At a baseball stadium, the players are getting ready to play an important game.

Critic's Corner

1. The baseball players worry about the bats they are choosing. Are the bats really that different?

2. Why do you think the players spend so much time and effort choosing the bats?

Mini-Dialog 6

Stage Setting

In a gym, observing workouts, we can learn much about ourselves and others.

Critic's Corner

1. How are the two bats in the gym like people?

2. How are the two bats alike? How are they different? At the end of their workouts, why would they say, "I am bats!"?

Mini-Dialog 7

Stage Setting

People's personalities can be strong—and different. The same thing is true of animals. Imagine the cat conversation below.

Critic's Corner

1. Do people ever act this way?

2. Besides humans, what other animals might compare their talents or their looks?

Mini-Dialog 8

Stage Setting

Samantha (Sam) *seems* to have lots of confidence. She's getting ready to go on stage.

Critic's Corner

1. What does the dialog above tell you about Samantha, the cat?

2. Is Samantha convinced that she can act?

Stage Setting

Casey is a super-athlete. People go to a game just to see Casey.

Critic's Corner

1. Why do you think people love super-athletes?

2. Who is your favorite athlete? Why?

Stage Setting

Casey comes up to bat. Everyone wonders what will happen.

Critic's Corner

1. Casey is a super-athlete. Do you think the announcer makes him nervous?

2. Is Casey able to concentrate on what he is doing? Explain why.

Mini-Dialog 11

Stage Setting

Super-athletes don't have much privacy. Casey is trying to go somewhere without being noticed.

Critic's Corner

1. Lots of people dream about becoming famous. Do you think Casey enjoys being famous?

2. How would you feel if you always had people watching you and judging you?

Mini-Dialog 12

The restaurant is advertising *Free Food.* That sounds too good to be true. Maybe there is a catch.

Critic's Corner

1. Are the people really paying for the food? How?

2. What does *scam* mean? Do you think this is a scam? Why?

Mini-Dialog 13

Stage Setting
Samantha loves acting in the cast. Tonight, she lets some others act with her.

Critic's Corner

1. Samantha is a great actress. Why does it take a whole cast, and not just one actor or actress, to create a good play or movie?

2. What do you think the cast members think of Samantha? Why?

Stage Setting

The play has ended, and the cast is leaving. They had a great time at the play.

Critic's Corner

1. The cast members have been working together. Now they want to go out together. Why do they like being together?

2. Why do you think they want to squeeze into the cab together?

Mini-Dialog 15

Stage Setting
Samantha has had an accident. She is not feeling well.

Critic's Corner

1. What do you think happened to Samantha?

2. Why do we visit people who have been hurt or who are sick?

Stage Setting

Sam and Mac have become friends. She's even agreed to go fishing with him.

Critic's Corner

1. Sam is still in a cast from her accident. How is Mac helping her?

2. When she no longer needs help, will she and Mac still be friends? Why do you think so?

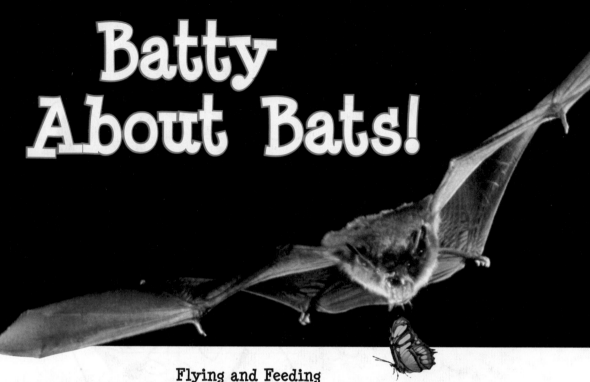

Batty About Bats!

Flying and Feeding

Bats can fly. They are the only **mammals** that
can fly. Bats use wings to fly. Skin connects the arms,
hands, and ankles of the bat. The skin makes wings.
Wings are important to a bat. They need them to fly
5 and find food.

Flying takes lots of energy, so bats eat a lot. Bats
eat half their weight each day. Bats eat a lot of things.
Some eat fruits and flowers. Some eat frogs and fish.
Some eat bugs. They eat mosquitoes and flies. They eat
10 moths and even termites!

Super Sonar

Did you think bats were blind? They are not. They
can see. Some even have good vision. Bats fly at night.
How do they find their way in the dark? Bats can "see"
with sound. They use sonar. Bats can "hear" where
15 they are. Bats cry out. We can't hear these sounds. Bats
find their way by listening to the echoes. Bats use other

clues too. They hear bugs buzzing in the air. They know where to find a good meal.

Hanging Out and Helping

20 Bats hang out. They hang upside down when they sleep. Some bats live in trees or buildings. Some bats live in caves. Millions of bats can live in one cave. Groups of bats living together are called **bat colonies**.

Bats "go to bat" for the Earth. Bats eat a lot of bugs. They save the plants that bugs like to eat. Without bats, 25 bugs could kill a lot of plants. Farmers can lose their farms. Millions of people would be hungry.

Bats also help plants grow. They scatter seeds. There is a fruit in Asia. It is a crop that brings in millions. What if there were no bats? This plant could 30 not grow. Farmers would lose cash.

Bats in Trouble

Today, bats are in danger from us. We destroy their homes. We **interfere** in their colonies. Some people have plans to help the bats. One plan shuts gates to old mines. This keeps people out, but it lets bats in. Some 35 chemicals kill bats. There is a plan to stop using these chemicals. These plans help everyone.

Scientists teach us about bats. Others help bats live. They count bat colonies. They study bats. What can you do for bats?

The Marianas flying fox eats fruit.

bat colonies
groups of bats living together

interfere
to get in the way of; disturb

A vampire bat goes for a "walk."

All photos © Merlin D. Tuttle Bat Conservation Intl.

ignorance
lack of knowledge

negligence
lack of care; lack of concern

40   "There is no point in finding out more about these creatures if we destroy them with **ignorance** and **negligence**," says one expert. "Bats need friends!"

Adapted from *Odyssey*, "Batty About Bats!" by Kathiann M. Kowalski, © by Carus Publishing Company. Reproduced with permission.

Answer It
Say the answer in a complete sentence.
See question 1.

1. Is a bat a mammal?
   Answer: Yes, a bat is a mammal.

2. Are all bats bug-eaters?

3. Are bats blind?

4. Are bats able to "see" with sound?

5. Are colonies where bats live?

6. Are bats dangerous to farmers?

7. Are bats helpful to crops?

8. Are bats in danger?

Bats in China

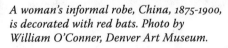

A woman's informal robe, China, 1875-1900, is decorated with red bats. Photo by William O'Conner, Denver Art Museum.

Photos ©Denver Art Museum

Something may be **honored** in one **culture** and despised in another. For example, Western people detest bats, but people in the East feel the opposite. In Europe and in early America, bats
5 suggested demons and evil. In much of Asia, on the other hand, bats are **prized**.

The Chinese people have prized bats for thousands of years. The Chinese word for bat is *fu* (pronounced *foo*), which sounds like their word for
10 luck, *fu.* Thousands of years ago, the Chinese looked for balance in the world around them. They saw life as a balance of opposites. They especially valued the

honored
respected, admired

culture
the language, customs, and beliefs of a group of people

prized
treasured, valued

balance between male and female. They saw the bat as a male sign and flowers and fruits as female signs.

15   In China, bats have always been common in art. The Chinese decorated many kinds of things with bats. They embroidered bats on clothing and painted bats on dishes. They carved bats and displayed them in their homes. They believed that this brought happiness

20 and long life. In their **shrines**, the Chinese used bats to honor their dead.

    Bats in Chinese art are often red, the color of happiness. A group of five bats shows that someone has lived a good life. The five bats stand for five

25 blessings. They are: health; long life; **prosperity**; love of **virtue**; and a peaceful, natural death. Sometimes, it is hard to see the bats in art. They may look more like flowers or leaves.

    Bats live long lives, much longer than any other

30 small mammal. We do not know why. We do know this. In China, bats mean wisdom and old age. May you have many bats!

shrines
sacred or spiritual places

prosperity
financial success

virtue
moral excellence, goodness

These Chinese characters for fu *mean "bat."*

Think About It

1. In Chinese, what does the word *fu* mean? Does it mean more than one thing?

2. Five bats stand for five blessings. What are they?

3. What did you learn about the life span of bats?

4. Why do you think Europeans revile, which means strongly dislike, bats?

5. Why do you think Asians revere, which means worship or honor, bats?

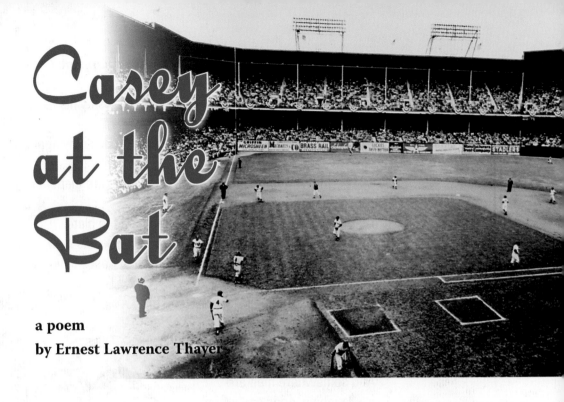

Casey at the Bat

a poem

by Ernest Lawrence Thayer

Summary: Casey was a **legendary** baseball player in the 1880s. He played for the Mudville team. The fans called him "Mighty Casey." This was because he always hit the ball so hard, and so far. He was a star! In
5 the 1880s, lots of people went to baseball games in the summer. A **famous** poem, "Casey at the Bat," tells the story of one special game.

This was the most important game of the season. The score was 4 to 2, and Mudville was behind. The
10 fans could only hope that Casey would get up to bat. If he did, they knew he could win it for Mudville! But there was little hope that Casey would get up to bat. The game was in the last inning. Mudville was behind. The 5,000 fans were losing hope.

15 But the two batters ahead of Casey got hits, and two runners were on base. Mighty Casey took his place at home plate. All the fans counted on him, because he was their star. Casey was ready to win for Mudville. Everybody knew he would pull through. With the first
20 two pitches, Casey made two **strikes**.

legendary
extremely well-known; mythical

famous
having widespread recognition

strikes
failures to hit pitched balls

These last lines of the poem tell you what happened next:

stern
grim, uninviting

They saw his face grow **stern** and cold; they saw his
    muscles strain,
And they knew that Casey wouldn't let that ball go by again.

sneer
a disrespectful
smile; smirk

The **sneer** is gone from Casey's lip; his teeth are clenched
5   in hate;
He pounds with cruel violence his bat upon the plate.
And now the pitcher holds the ball and now he lets it go,
And now the air is shattered by the force of Casey's blow.

Oh! Somewhere in this favored land the
10   sun is shining bright;
The band is playing somewhere, and
    somewhere hearts are light,
And somewhere men are
    laughing, and somewhere
15   children shout;
But there is no joy in
    Mudville—Mighty
    Casey has struck out.

Think About It

1. What was the name of the team that Casey played for?

2. The fans called him "Mighty Casey." How did he get that name?

3. "They saw his face grow stern and cold . . ." Why would Casey have this kind of look on his face?

4. In the last stanza (the last 10 lines), the poem creates contrast. What is the contrast between the first seven lines and the last three lines in the stanza?

5. Why do you think the poet used this contrast?

At Bat

by Jacqueline Hechtkopf

The pitcher throws the ball
and decision splits the air.
Wait for the next one or swing?

The right choice mixed with
5 luck and muscle means
the crowd will stand
and cheer.

Forget wrong decisions
returning in silence
10 to sulk on the bench.

That was last time
and the time before.

Keep your eye on the ball
and send fear sailing
15 over the fence.

From *Cricket* © by Carus Publishing Company.
Reproduced with permission.

Think About It

1. Everybody has made poor choices. Everybody has made bad decisions. When we do, we can choose again: try once more or "sulk on the bench." What does the poet really mean by "sulk on the bench"?

2. What is the poet recommending here?

3. Is there a way to know if we are making the "right choice"?

4. Are we able to forget what has happened in the past? What will happen to our future if we always let the past control our decisions?

5. Can you think of how this advice might help you? How it might help someone you know?

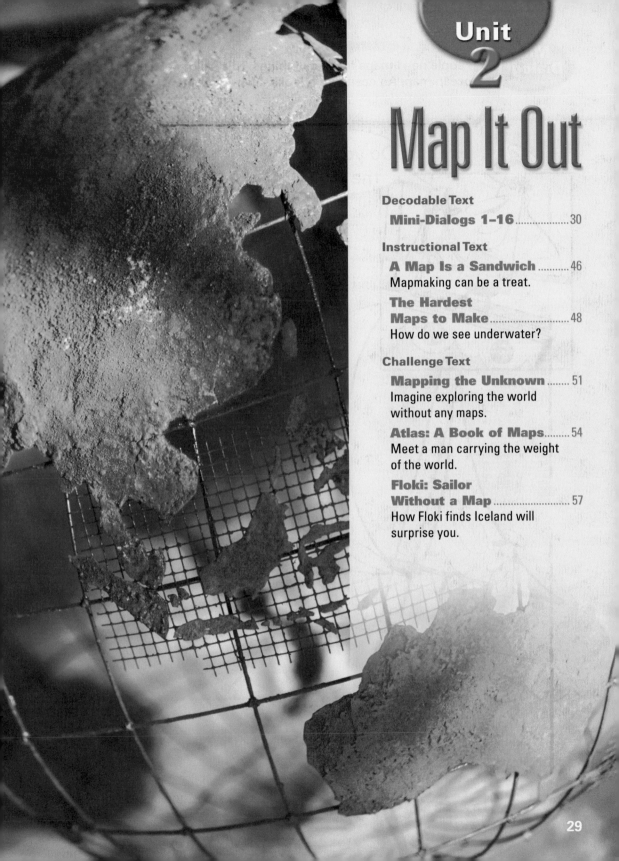

Map It Out

Stage Setting

People need maps for lots of things. This sailor needs an ocean map. An ocean map looks different from a land map.

Critic's Corner

1. If the parrot has the sailor's map, how will the sailor find his way?

2. Discuss this statement: *A map is more important at sea than it is on land.* Do you agree or disagree? Why?

Stage Setting

Two scientists have just arrived at the airport and gotten into a cab. They are headed to an important meeting at a science lab in a large city.

Critic's Corner

1. These scientists can understand all kinds of difficult ideas and they have a lot to think about. Why did they forget the map to the lab?

2. Have you ever forgotten something important when you were busy?

Stage Setting

Sometimes, we are misled. See how easily these aliens are misled.

Critic's Corner

1. What confused the aliens?

2. What would have happened if they had a globe instead of a map?

Stage Setting

When we don't have information about a subject, we can draw the wrong conclusion. These aliens seem to have drawn the wrong conclusion.

Critic's Corner

1. Why did the aliens conclude that the CAT scan was a diagnostic machine for cats?

2. What does CAT scan (sometimes called CT scan) stand for?

Stage Setting

It's a good thing to try to appreciate the work of a sculptor. Sometimes, abstract sculpture is difficult to understand if you do not know the sculptor's intent.

Critic's Corner

1. These people were trying to understand the sculptor's work. What might have made it easier for them to understand the sculptor's work?

2. Is it hard to understand art? Why?

Stage Setting

Paintings can be abstract, and artists may require us to think about what we are seeing. Abstract art is interesting because different people see different things in the same painting.

Critic's Corner

1. Compare and contrast representational (realistic) art and abstract art. How are they alike? How are they different?

2. Which do you prefer? Why?

Stage Setting

Like people, animals have different kinds of talent. Some are more athletic than others. Some are super-runners.

Critic's Corner

1. The people are amazed by the dog's running ability. Have you ever known an animal that had some special talent?

2. Describe the special abilities of some animals.

Stage Setting

Sometimes, we get into contests that are silly. Think about the following competition and why it is silly.

Critic's Corner

1. Have you ever felt like you were competing out of your league? What put you in that position?

2. In school, is there a subject that is easier for you than for others?

Stage Setting

Life sometimes offers us the unexpected. Usually, we're not ready to handle it, because we didn't see it coming.

Critic's Corner

1. The fisherman didn't get the crabs he was fishing for. Was he upset?

2. What do you expect the fisherman to do next?

Stage Setting

We all have fears. Sometimes, our fears are unreasonable.

Critic's Corner

1. Maybe elephants aren't really afraid of ants. But they do have fears. Explain why we sometimes have unreasonable fears.

2. Remember when you were a small child. Think of some unreasonable fear that you had. Why do you think you feared it?

Stage Setting

Everybody should have healthy fears. These scientists realize the danger they have encountered.

Critic's Corner

1. Can we ever feel 100 percent safe?

2. Think of three professions that require healthy fear. What is the difference between a healthy fear and an unhealthy fear?

Stage Setting

Sometimes, we use the wrong tool to do a job. Sometimes, we expect others to do the impossible.

Critic's Corner

1. Sometimes, we try to do a job without the right tools. Think of a situation when something has failed because the right tools weren't used.

2. Can we think of people's talents as tools?

Stage Setting

Each of us has different interests. It's always good to find others who share our interests.

Critic's Corner

1. These people share the interest of acting. What interest would you like to pursue?

2. Give three reasons for your interest. How could you pursue your interest?

Stage Setting

Mini-Dialog 14

Of course, there are no genies, but old stories said that genies could grant special wishes.

Critic's Corner

1. Why do you think the alien was happy to go to the past?

2. Is there a time in the past that you would like to visit?

Stage Setting

There are thousands of strange animals that people seldom see. Zoos are wonderful places, as long as the animals are well cared for. But this space zoo is weird.

Critic's Corner

1. The aliens are visiting a zoo unlike any on Earth. What is different about their space zoo?

2. Are you aware of any creatures on Earth that are as bizarre as these creatures?

Stage Setting

Even aliens find unusual creatures in the space zoo. Think about what causes their surprise.

Is that a bat in pants?

Yes. And that asp naps on a raft.

Look! The clams are in a cab!

This is a blast!

Critic's Corner

1. What do the aliens find unusual about the animals in the space zoo?

2. Comedy writers for TV, movies, and books have to think about what makes a situation funny. What do you think turns an ordinary situation into a comedy?

A Map Is a Sandwich

Making a map is like making a sandwich. Think about it. A sandwich has layers. First, there is a layer of bread, and then there is a layer of mustard. Add lettuce, meat, and cheese. Last but not least, add a top
5 layer of bread.

Stacy and Diana are cartographers. They use facts to make maps. They use facts from the sky. These facts come from **satellites**. They get facts from land. These facts come from **surveys**. Pictures of black lines come
10 to them. Diana and Stacy use computers to turn the lines into maps.

First, they study the lines. The lines show places. Stacy and Diana ask questions. What lines are **borders** and what lines are roads? What lines are rivers, and
15 what lines are forests?

Stacy explains. "When we make maps, we work in layers. We begin with the lines. They give us layers of information. It's like making a sandwich. Say you're making a map. You start with a layer of land. You add
20 layers of forests, rivers, and roads. The last layer adds names of cities and towns."

satellites

objects in space that go around planets to get facts

surveys

studies using special tools to find the size and shape of areas of land

borders

lines that mark the edge of an area

Next, they add color. Diana tells why. "Important things have to stand out. They need bright colors. If you are making a map of state parks, show the parks
25 in bright green."

Last, the cartographers make a **key**. The key shows symbols in different colors. A tiny tent shows a campground. A tiny airplane shows an airport. Major highways are **bold** red lines. A small road is a row of
30 black dashes. The key shows what the symbols mean. When the key is easy to understand, the map is good. Stacy explains, "You want everybody to understand it. Not everybody is good with maps. When is a map *really* good? It's really good when you don't have to look
35 at the key!"

"No map is perfect," Stacy says. "There is a big problem. Maps are flat, but the Earth is round." Stacy is right. Maps have **limits**. But without them, we'd be lost!

key
a list of symbols used on a map

bold
darkened letters or words

limits
things that prevent something from being perfect or complete

Adapted from *Appleseeds*, "A Map Is a Sandwich" by Jeanne Miller, © by Carus Publishing Company. Reproduced with permission.

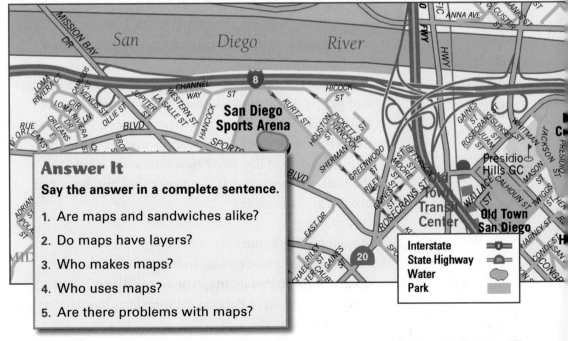

Answer It

Say the answer in a complete sentence.

1. Are maps and sandwiches alike?
2. Do maps have layers?
3. Who makes maps?
4. Who uses maps?
5. Are there problems with maps?

Interstate
State Highway
Water
Park

The Hardest Maps to Make

A Hard Job

Making maps is fun. We can map land, mountains, **plains**, and valleys. Can we map water? We can map **ponds**, **lakes**, and **rivers**. Can we map oceans? Oceans are hard to map because they are deep. We
5 can't see the bottom. It is dark at the bottom. We can't take pictures. Fish can't talk to us. They can't share their travels.

Under the ocean, there are mountains, valleys, and plains. How do we know? More than 100 years
10 ago, people wanted to know. They wanted to map the ocean. They went out in ships and put long lines into the water. They tried to see how far it was to the bottom. It worked if the water was not deep. But oceans are very deep!

Mapping With Sonar

15 We found a better way to map land under the ocean. Sonar helps us map the ocean floor. What animal uses sonar? Bats do. Mapmakers studied bats.

plains
large, flat areas of land without trees

ponds
small bodies of still water

lakes
large bodies of still water

rivers
large streams of flowing water

Bats use sound to "see" in the dark. We found that we could use sonar too.

20 Sonar is a "sound camera." It turns sounds into pictures. Instead of using light, sonar uses sound. It can "see" into deep places. It measures the distance by counting the time it takes for echoes to come back from the bottom of the ocean. Echoes sound differently

25 in deep places than in shallow places. The computer helps because it turns sounds into pictures! The pictures show the bottom.

But sonar is not perfect. It is slow. We have worked for more than 50 years, and only parts of the oceans

30 are mapped. What if we use the best sonar? It would

©E. Paul Oberlander, Woods Hole Oceanographic Institution

still take over 100 years. The ocean is about 70 percent of the Earth's surface! Another problem is cost. Sonar costs a lot.

Ocean Mapping Today

Today, ocean maps are better. Scientists had an
35 idea to use sonar and satellite pictures *together*. Sonar and satellite pictures used together make better maps. Scientists also use new vehicles. These vehicles can work on the ocean floor. They don't need people to drive them. They take pictures of what is underneath
40 the sea.

frontier
an area that is being explored

Mapping Earth's Last Frontier

Today's ocean maps give facts we need. These maps help us find fish and minerals. They measure the ocean's flow. The ocean's flow **affects** our weather. It affects shipping and travel. We have more facts to
45 learn. The ocean is a final frontier for mapmakers.

affects
causes a change; has an impact on

Adapted from *Appleseeds*, "Oceans, Mapping Earth's Last Frontier"
by Sherrill Kushner, © by Carus Publishing Company.
Reproduced with permission.

Answer It
Say the answer in a complete sentence.

1. Who learned about using sound and echoes from bats?

2. Do echoes from all places in the ocean sound alike?

3. Are there limits to sonar?

4. Are scientists today using only sonar to map oceans?

5. Do mapmakers already have all the facts about oceans?

Mapping the Unknown

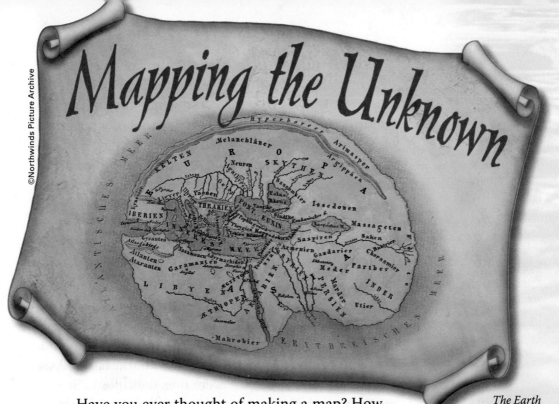

The Earth according to Herodotus.

Have you ever thought of making a map? How would you begin? Try standing at your front door and drawing a map of your block. It is hard because you can't see the whole block. Today, we can make exact
5 maps because we use pictures from airplanes and satellites. But making maps has not always been easy.

Early mapmakers had to trust what they could see with their own eyes. They had to rely on things that travelers, explorers, and native people told them. A
10 traveler might say that a city lay where a river flowed into the sea. Sailors might tell of islands off a coast or maybe they recalled a bay near some cliffs. Mapmakers drew these things on their maps.

Early mapmakers did not have exact ways to
15 measure the distance between places. Instead, they had to find out how long it took to go from one location to another. Travelers would tell how much time they had spent on their trips. Mapmakers learned how long it took to walk to a certain place or get there
20 by horse. They counted how many days it took to sail there by ship.

The first mapmakers used the sun and stars to map distant places. Was the place in the East, where the sun rises? Or was it in the West, where the sun sets?
25 Sailors knew about the winds. They told of winds that blew from the north and pushed ships toward islands in the south. They talked about winds from the east that carried them to a western shore.

Early maps were full of mistakes. There were no
30 satellites or airplanes. With no way to take pictures from the sky, judging distance was a big problem. For example, **Columbus** believed the world was much smaller. In 1492, he sailed west and landed on an island. He thought he was in Asia, but Asia was
35 thousands of miles farther away!

Sometimes, travelers misled mapmakers. Some told of a land bridge between Africa and southeastern Asia. Others said the Americas were one **continent**. Some maps showed places as explorers hoped they would
40 be. For example, they showed a sea passage to China through the middle of North America, but of course no such passage exists.

Travelers also described creatures they had seen. Sometimes they **exaggerated**. Whales became "sea
45 monsters," while lizards and snakes became "**dragons**." These fantastic creatures were **intriguing**, and mapmakers added them to their maps.

Many people feared the unknown. What lay beyond the mountains? What lived at the edge of the
50 sea? Perhaps there were dragons! Mapmakers had to include unexplored land and seas on their maps. They **indicated** these places with pictures of dragons and sea monsters.

Today, we have airplanes and satellites. We have
55 filled in almost all of the mysterious spaces. What is left to map? The bottoms of the oceans are not completely mapped. Could there be dragons down there?

Adapted from *Appleseeds*, "Here Be Dragons" by Natalie Rosinsky,
© by Carus Publishing Company. Reproduced with permission.

Columbus
famous Italian explorer

continent
a major landmass

exaggerated
overstated or magnified

dragons
mythical, winged monsters

intriguing
very interesting; fascinating

indicated
served as a sign of something; showed

Dragons Are:

➤ legendary reptiles

➤ symbols of destruction, evil, death, and sin in some cultures

➤ credited with having powers necessary to understand the secrets of the Earth in other cultures

➤ regarded by Chinese people as a symbol of good fortune

©Northwinds Picture Archive

Think About It

1. What makes maps in today's world more accurate than maps in the past?

2. When ancient travelers wanted to know the distance between places, what did they do?

3. Ancient travelers judged the distance between places by how much time it took to go from one place to another. What types of transportation could you use in today's world to measure travel times?

4. Why do you think travelers exaggerated about what they had seen rather than provide exact descriptions?

5. Columbus thought he had sailed to Asia when he had actually sailed only to an island. What do you think Columbus would do if he knew that he had not reached Asia?

6. Why do you think people feared the unknown? When have you been fearful in an unfamiliar situation?

ATLAS: A BOOK OF MAPS

Where do we look for maps? We look in an atlas, of course. Have you ever wondered why a book of maps is called an atlas? What is the origin of this word, and how is it related to maps? This is the story

5 of an ancient Greek named Atlas. By the time you come to the end, you'll understand why Atlas' name is **associated** with maps.

associated
related, connected

THE STORY OF ATLAS: A GREEK MYTH

An atlas is a book of maps, but the word *atlas* also has a different meaning. It was someone's name. Here's
10 the story of the first Atlas.

The ancient Greeks told tales about giant beings called Titans. One of these giants was named Atlas. The Titans once fought against the Greek gods, so the gods punished them. Atlas' punishment was to hold
15 the sky up on his shoulders. He balanced the sky on his shoulders for many, many years.

Once, Atlas almost got free. A brave hero named Hercules paid him a visit. Hercules needed to locate some golden apples, and only Atlas knew where they
20 grew. Atlas said, "I'll fetch the apples for you if you'll hold the sky up while I'm gone."

Hercules was very strong, almost as strong as a Titan. He agreed to hold the sky up while Atlas went for the apples, but it was tough work. When Atlas
25 returned with the fruit, he saw Hercules sweating and groaning underneath the weight of the sky. Who would want to take back a job like that? Atlas thought, "I could leave Hercules here and walk away. Then I would be free forever."

30 Hercules **realized** what Atlas was thinking, so Hercules thought of a trick. "This sky is very **uncomfortable**!" he told Atlas. "Hold it up for a minute while I put a pad on my shoulders. Then I'll hold it up again." Unaware of the trick, Atlas placed the
35 sky back on his own shoulders.

realized
came to understand; sensed

uncomfortable
feeling discomfort

The minute Hercules was free, he ran away. Atlas had to keep holding up the sky forever. Eventually, he turned into stone mountains—the Atlas Mountains in northwestern Africa. Even now, Atlas still seems to 40 carry the sky on his shoulders.

About 500 years ago, a great cartographer named Gerardus Mercator created a book of maps. In the book, he told the tale of Atlas. Ever since then, a book of maps has been called an atlas.

From *Appleseeds*, "The Story of Atlas" by Judy Rosenbaum,
© by Carus Publishing Company. Reproduced with permission.

Think About It

1. What do we call a book of maps?

2. Who were the Titans?

3. How did Hercules trick Atlas?

4. How do you think Atlas felt when Hercules outsmarted him?

5. What might have happened if Atlas didn't fall for Hercules' trick?

6. Have you ever had a particularly unpleasant job or chore? What are some of the ways of coping with an unfavorable task?

Floki: Sailor Without a Map

Floki lived in **Norway** hundreds of years ago. He was a dreamer who longed to sail to faraway lands. There was one beautiful place called **Iceland** that Floki especially wanted to see, but how could he get there? There were no
5   maps to guide him, and he had no ship to carry him there.

After many years passed, Floki at last had a ship and a crew, and he was ready to make the long journey to Iceland. He knew it was in the West, so he and his crew set out in that direction, traveling over a **vast**, gray ocean.
10 Their open boat gave them little protection from the cold weather and rough seas. Worse than that, Floki still had no map. How could he find Iceland without a map?

Floki was a clever man, and he had a plan. He had brought a cage of ravens on the ship. After he had been at
15 sea for many days, he freed one bird. It flew back toward Norway and didn't return to the ship. What did that mean? Birds fly to the nearest land, so Floki knew that the nearest land was the place he had just left. That wasn't

Norway
a country of Northern Europe

Iceland
an island nation in the North Atlantic

vast
very large, immense

The Norsemen and their raven pilot.

the route to Iceland. Soon, Floki
20 released another raven, but this time
it came right back to the ship. This
continued for weeks. Whenever a
raven was freed, it flew back to the
ship. No land was near.
25   Months passed. The men were
hungry and cold, and Floki was
getting worried. He had to find
Iceland soon! One dark day, Floki
freed two birds. When they flew
30 ahead and did not come back, Floki
knew land had to be nearby. He
stayed the course, and a few days
later, land was in sight. His dream
had come true! Floki had finally
35 reached Iceland!

Adapted from *Appleseeds*, "Here Be
Dragons" by Natalie Rosinsky, © by Carus
Publishing Company. Reproduced with
permission.

Think About It

1. Who was Floki? Where did he live?

2. What was Floki's dream? Why was his dream such a challenge?

3. What did Floki take with him on his trip? Why?

4. For weeks, ravens were freed but returned to the ship. No land was near. How do you think Floki and his men felt about how far they were from land?

5. If you were a sailor on Floki's ship, would you sign on for another journey with him? Why or why not?

6. Floki's dream came true. What is your greatest dream? What is the greatest challenge to making it come true?

Unit 3

Dig It!

59

Stage Setting

An old saying says, "Don't count your chickens before they're hatched." As you read this cartoon, think of ways it might apply to these people.

Critic's Corner

1. What is a *draft*? Make a list of work that must be finished before a film can be produced.

2. What are these two planning? Are their plans realistic?

Stage Setting

We often misunderstand what is said. Sometimes, it's because we're thinking of a different meaning for a word.

Critic's Corner

1. What did each bat think? What caused their misunderstanding?

2. Misunderstanding can result in funny situations. Can it also cause bad situations? Give examples.

Stage Setting

Knowing your direction is important. Sometimes, maps are critical. Decide whether these people have planned well enough for their trip.

Critic's Corner

1. These flyers didn't have a map and they got lost. Have you ever been lost? Remember the situation.

2. Have you ever felt lost? Remember that situation. What is the difference between *being* lost and *feeling* lost?

Mini-Dialog 4

Stage Setting

Sometimes, we are called on to do heroic deeds that we don't think we could do.

Critic's Corner

1. Beavers are known as hard workers. What do you know about these animals?

2. Do you think that an animal, like a beaver, could intentionally do a heroic deed? Or do you think that all animals in a species are exactly the same?

Stage Setting

Two ladies are shopping. They're looking at purses in the window of a boutique. Watch for the *pun* that follows.

Critic's Corner

1. A *pun* is a humorous use of a word or phrase to suggest more than one meaning. What is the pun in this cartoon?

2. Why do you think people often groan when they hear a pun?

Stage Setting

Sometimes, the unknown frightens us. Watch what happens when two people face the unknown in a dark, unfamiliar attic.

Critic's Corner

1. What is the most frightening thing these two could actually encounter in the grandmother's attic?

2. Think of a time you have been in an unfamiliar place, facing an unknown situation. Why are we less sure of ourselves in unfamiliar situations?

Stage Setting

Let's think about what *perspective* means. It means a point of view. Things look different from different points of view. Sometimes, it's good to see how others view things.

Critic's Corner

1. What do you suspect the ants think of the Big Dig?

2. Should the ants compare their digging skill with the machines used for the dig in Boston?

Stage Setting

Depending on where you live, different words have different meanings for you. These people are from Boston, Massachusetts.

Critic's Corner

1. Does the fact that these two men are from Boston give you a clue as to what they mean by the Big Dig? (You will read about the Big Dig later in this unit.)

2. What are their perspectives on the ants' Big Dig?

Stage Setting

Museums contain art masterpieces and science treasures. During the day, people visit, but at night strange things happen.

What are they? Who are they? Can they stand?

They can stand. They grandstand. Are they big, plastic plants?

Are they big, abstract rabbits?

They are big, misfit dinosaurs!

Hmmm. They are trim.

NATURAL H

Critic's Corner

1. The statues represent art; the dinosaurs represent science. Throughout history, people have argued about which is more important: science or art. Why?

2. Which do you think is more important? Give three specific reasons.

Stage Setting

One way that people play with words is a type of joke, called a *pun*. A pun is a humorous use of a word or phrase, suggesting more than one meaning. Watch for the pun here.

Critic's Corner

1. What is the pun in this cartoon? Why would it make some people groan?

2. Puns can be clever, but they're sometimes called *corny*. Why would we call something corny when it has absolutely nothing to do with corn? Go to the library at school and ask the librarian to help you find the answer.

Stage Setting

Every day, unexpected events slow us down. Let's watch our friendly aliens, and see what their *perspective* is. How do they view this situation?

Critic's Corner

1. Imagine the perspective of outside observers who know nothing about our transportation system. What are the aliens thinking?

2. What does *road rage* mean? Why do people become so angry about things they cannot control?

Stage Setting

Could dead dinosaurs have a perspective of their own? Watch what happens at our favorite dig site, and decide for yourself.

Critic's Corner

1. Compare and contrast the viewpoints of the paleontologists and the dinosaurs. How are they alike? How are they different?

2. Why do the angel dinosaurs call the scientists *bandits*? Are they really stealing?

Stage Setting

Some aliens are trying to figure out earthlings. Their perspective is based on the first things they see.

Critic's Corner

1. What conclusions have the aliens reached about earthlings? How were their perspectives formed?

2. Are our own perspectives formed based on things we see? Could these perspectives turn into prejudice?

Stage Setting

Many of us like participating in sports. Some who participate make excuses when they do not do well. Decide what you think about the participants in this wacky track meet.

That rabbit can sprint! It ran past the pig and the asp.

This track is bad. It is sand.

That pig is past the asp!!!

Rabbit wins! Too bad! The asp has had a mishap! The asp is last.

Critic's Corner

1. The asp came in last in the track meet. What do you think her mishap might have been?

2. What did the pig complain about? Was the condition of the track worse for her than for the rabbit or the asp?

Stage Setting

Some people spend years, and continue working, because their goals are important. As you read this cartoon, think about these paleontologists' goals.

Critic's Corner

1. These two scientists are clearly disappointed. What might they have been looking for?

2. Think of a time when you have wanted something, have expected it, and yet have been disappointed.

Stage Setting

We often look at successful people and think of their lives as always busy. These two paleontologists can teach us something.

Critic's Corner

1. Do you think it is a good idea for these paleontologists to take a break from their work? Why?

2. What do you like to do when you take a break?

Africa Digs

Dr. Paul Sereno digs dinosaur bones. He gets a thrill when he digs up the bones of dinosaurs who lived thousands of years ago. In 1997, Dr. Sereno led a dig to **Niger**, Africa. He took 18 scientists with him.
5 The Touareg tribe helped his team look for bones. The Touareg people live in Niger. They know their **desert** land best. They know where to look for bones.

Niger

a country of west Africa

The dig was a success. Dr. Sereno's team had a fantastic find. They found a new dinosaur. The
10 Touareg told them a legend about a very big animal. They call it *Jobar.* The Touareg showed them where to look for the bones. The scientists named the dinosaur *Jobaria.* It means giant. How did they dig up the *Jobaria?* Let's follow the dig step by step.

desert

a dry place with little rainfall

Step 1: We've Got One!

15 The Touareg lead the team to a special place. Bones stick out of desert rock. The Touareg tell the scientists their legend. These bones belong to the giant beast, *Jobar.*

Step 2: Digging In

20 The dig begins. They use hammers, chisels, and drills. They work for 10 weeks. A huge skeleton **emerges**. It has been buried for 135 million years! Fifteen tons of rock cover it. The team carefully takes the bones
25 from the rock.

emerges

comes out of; appears

The Touareg tribe helped the team.

Step 3: Wrap It Up

They have to make "jackets" to protect the **fossils**. They cover the bones with paper or foil. They cut burlap strips and dip them in plaster. They wrap each bone with the burlap strips. First, they cover one side. The
30 strip dries into a hard jacket. Then, they cover the other side. They number the jackets. They **log** each number in the dig's **log** book.

fossils

the bones or the marks left by animals and plants from a long time ago

Step 4: Move It Out

The team must take the bones to their lab in Chicago. Twenty tons of bones have to be moved. Some
35 weigh over 500 pounds. They have no machines to move them. They use a tripod, pulleys, rope, and a chain. They load the bones onto trucks. They drive 1,000 miles to a port in Ghana. They put the bones on a ship, which
40 takes them across the Atlantic. Then, the bones are shipped to Chicago.

log

1. to write down what happened
2. a record of what happened

Step 5: Unwrap It

The team carefully opens each piece and cleans each
45 bone. They match the numbers on the jackets to the numbers in the dig's log book. The bones are put in the right order. Now it's time to rebuild the skeleton.

Step 6: Clean 'Em Up

50 This step takes two years and hundreds of hours. They use dental tools, tiny jackhammers, and chemicals. The work is careful and
55 precise. They have to clean

Dr. Paul Sereno and his team at the African dig site.

Dr. Paul Sereno examines the dinosaur bones.

more than 200 bones. These bones came from the adult *Jobaria*. But they have some other bones as well. These are from young *Jobaria*. They clean these bones too.

Step 7: And the Missing Pieces?

They have good luck! They have almost all of the
60 adult's bones. What about the ones that are missing? They fill in the missing bones by making them out of foam and clay.

Step 8: Make a Plan

All of the bones are clean. The missing bones are made. At last, they can make a model. From it, they
65 create a blueprint. This is the plan to rebuild the skeleton. First, they lay out the tail bones. They place them in order. Next, they study how to put the bones back together. Now, they can see the huge size of the dinosaur.

Step 9: Copy the Fossils

70   *Jobaria's* bones are too heavy and **fragile** to put together. Dr. Sereno's team wants to display the dinosaur. What can they do? They copy the skeleton. They make molds. They create copies of the bones.

Step 10: Stack It Up

75   They attach the casts of the bones to a steel frame. The hard steel frame is covered by the bones.

Finally: Share the Discovery!

    They paint the casts to look like the real fossils. They are white with tints of
80 green and red. These colors come from copper and iron in the soil. At last, they pose the dinosaur. It looks so real! You can almost hear that dinosaur roar!

Adapted from *Odyssey*, "Finding the Pieces…
and Putting Them Back Together Again"
by Michelle Laliberte, © by Carus Publishing
Company. Reproduced with permission.

Did You Know?

The ancient Greeks did not know about dinosaurs. But they had a word, *deinos*, that meant "terrible" or "monstrous" and a word, *saur*, that meant "lizard." In the 1800s when scientists began to study fossilized bones of these beasts, they used the Greek words to name them and gave us the word *dinosaur.* Why is "terrible lizard" a good name for these animals?

Answer It
Say the answer in a complete sentence.

1. Who led the dig in Niger, Africa?
2. Who helped the leader with the dig?
3. What did the dig team make to protect the fossils?
4. What did they use to load the bones onto trucks?
5. What did they use to clean the bones?
6. What did the team do if bones were missing?
7. What did the team create to help them build the skeleton?
8. What was the skeleton frame made out of?

The Big Dig

Zakim Bridge

Traffic is a big problem in big cities. Millions of people use the roads to get to work and school. Municipal and city governments have the responsibility to maintain bridges, roads, and tunnels; but, as time
5 passes, all structures suffer wear and tear. Sometimes, *everything* needs fixing. In Boston, Massachusetts, that is what happened, and the solution was called the "Big Dig."

Road congestion in Boston was so fierce in the 1990s that for up to 10 hours of the day, traffic could only crawl.
10 The city had a high accident rate, added to noise and air pollution. The metropolitan area needed new bridges, roads, and tunnels—what is called "the infrastructure."

overhaul

a large repair job; renovation

Boston began the biggest traffic **overhaul** ever attempted. Officials knew it would take years to finish.
15 This is what they had to do:

Overhaul Boston's Central Artery—
the heart of its highway system.

1. Construct a new bridge and tunnel system.
2. Build the structures in the same spots where the original ones are now.
3. Avoid closing any roads during construction.

landfill

a site where dirt has filled in low-lying ground

20 4. Build under water, through water, and in unstable **landfill** conditions.
5. Dodge **foundations** of fragile historic buildings.
6. Dodge skyscrapers.

foundations

supportive bases on which buildings stand

7. Avoid generating too much dust or noise—don't
25 disturb the people of Boston.

What could the city do?

Some might say that the task was impossible, but not to the **civil engineers** who managed the Big Dig. Fred Salvucci was born in Boston and grew up to be a civil engineer. He specified that the network of roads had to
30 be wider, but it was not possible on the ground level to go around the great mass of buildings that made up the city's skyline. Fred Salvucci suggested sinking the entire highway system underground.

civil engineers
people who design and build public bridges, highways, and other structures

How did they do it?

How would they realize that radical vision? Engineers
35 met in the early 1980s and labored over the design. They planned the biggest, most **complex** road project in U.S. history. Construction began in 1991. It captured the attention of the world.

Some people said the Big Dig was a big mess. It
40 cost ten billion dollars more than planned. And tragedy struck in 2006, when a driver was killed by falling concrete from a newly opened tunnel.

Major public projects, such as the construction of airports and government buildings, often draw
45 controversy. Huge amounts of money are at stake, and politicians must overcome their conflicting views and work cooperatively toward important goals.

complex
complicated, intricate

circumnavigate
to go all the way around; circle

The Big Dig Facts

- The Big Dig used lots of concrete. How much? Enough to build a 3-foot-wide sidewalk from Boston to San Francisco and back three times.

- More than 5,000 men and women worked on the Big Dig every day.

- The Big Dig used lots of steel. How much? Enough to make a 1-inch-thick steel bar. How long would the steel bar be? The bar could **circumnavigate** the Earth's equator.

Workers poured tons of concrete.

Southbay Interchange

I-93 North runs through a tunnel.

After critical repairs, the 20-year Big Dig project appears to have
50 triumphed. Within a 7.5-mile area, Boston's Central Artery/Tunnel Project includes three different types of tunnels, the largest cable bridge in the world, and 161 lane-miles of
55 new highway. Now, Boston has almost 150 acres of new parks and open space.

Adapted from *Odyssey*, "Big Dig" by Laurie Ann Toupin,
© by Carus Publishing Company. Reproduced with permission.

Think About It

1. Where did the Big Dig take place?

2. What was the purpose of the Big Dig?

3. Who was Fred Salvucci? What was his profession? What important suggestion did Fred Salvucci make?

4. Pretend that you are Salvucci. Give reasons why putting the highway underground is a good idea.

5. Because of the Big Dig, the city of Boston has many new parks. What might be the benefits and the problems associated with these new parks?

6. Think of a problem facing your community. How would you solve it?

Dig This!

Shureice cleans dinosaur bones.

When Shureice Kornegay, a 10th grader from Chicago, Illinois, went on a paleontological expedition, she gathered historic bones and valuable new experiences. Here, she recounts the events of her three-
5   week adventure.

I was excited! I was going on a real dig! Would we find dinosaur bones? I was a normal 10th grader, but for three weeks, I got to be someone special—a junior paleontologist. I got to hike in the Rockies; visit the
10 Lewis and Clark Museum; make discoveries on Egg Mountain; and even do some bird-watching. Best of all, I made new friends and had lots of fun.

Arriving

Dr. Paul Sereno and his wife, Gabrielle Lyon, have a special program called Project Exploration. I, Shureice
15 Kornegay of Chicago, was chosen to participate along with a group of other students. We traveled to Choteau, Montana, and that first day headed for the Old Trail Museum. Here, we learned our assignments. Paul and Gabrielle showed us around the museum. They told us
20 we would be spending lots of time there.

Montana dig site

Beginning

I could hardly believe it! I was a junior paleontologist on my first field trip! I didn't know what to expect. I had never been to Montana, but I was up for the challenge.

Digging

25   We headed over to Pine Butte, which was an area of badlands. It was a large, hilly open space. Badlands are **barren** areas with rough, **eroded** ridges, peaks, and **mesas**. Here, the bones we were looking for may be exposed above ground. We split up into two groups,
30 and my group went prospecting. Our job was to look around for bones. We climbed up a steep hill. We took out our pickaxes and dental tools. (Yes, we had dental tools.) We searched for a starting spot. I couldn't wait to start digging! I knew we'd find those dino bones!

barren
without plant life; unproductive

eroded
worn away

mesas
wide, flat-topped hills

Discovering

35   We found a lot of calcite, a bright, brittle rock that looks just like bone. We learned a trick to tell the difference between bone and rock. This was the "lick test." When you lick a real bone, your tongue sticks to it because bone is **porous**. Does that sound
40   disgusting? It isn't really. Using the "lick test," we found lots of small bones that we put into sealed plastic bags. I found the tip of a rib! We learned that these ancient bones are very fragile. We used a chemical comparable to super glue to hold the rib tip together.

> **porous**
> having many small holes or pores

Climbing

45   During the trip, we also went on an 8-mile hike into the Rockies. I led the way for a bit. We filled up our water bottles at a freshwater spring along the way. Our destination was over 7,000 feet in altitude. We ended the day with a barbecue at the museum and learned
50   about tribes that had inhabited Montana hundreds of years ago. We told some scary stories to see who we could spook. That night, we roasted marshmallows.

We also got to visit Egg Mountain, a place where many skeletons of the dinosaur *Maiasaura* were found.
55   Nests and babies were found there too. *Maiasaura* was about 30 feet long and lived in the late Cretaceous Period. At this site, we learned to recognize small fragments of eggshell. These were dark, almost black, in the **sediment**. **Prolific** bone beds, like the one
60   at Egg Mountain, show that the adult *Maiasaura* dinosaurs took care of their young.

> **sediment**
> a dirt-like substance consisting of tiny pieces of rock

> **prolific**
> having large amounts; abundant

Saying Good-bye

I felt a sense of sad gratitude as I said farewell to my two adult mentors and my new buddies. But after a stint as a paleontologist, who knows what's next for me.
65   Whatever it is, I'll be up for it!

Adapted from *Odyssey*, "Fantastic Journeys: Dig This!" by Shureice Kornegay, © by Carus Publishing Company. Reproduced with permission.

Think About It

1. Who is Shureice Kornegay? Where is her home? Where did she go on a trip?

2. How did Shureice describe the Badlands of Montana?

3. Why is calcite easily confused with bone? What is the name of the trick that the students used to distinguish between calcite and bone?

4. During the trip, the students went on a hike into the Rocky Mountains. What might have been the positive and negative memories of this particular experience?

5. Shureice's trip allowed her to explore a subject that was interesting to her. If you could choose a subject to explore on a trip, where would you go? What would you explore?

6. Shureice kept a journal of her trip. You have just finished reading her journal. Have you ever kept a journal? Do you have a special time ahead of you, one that you'd like to remember?

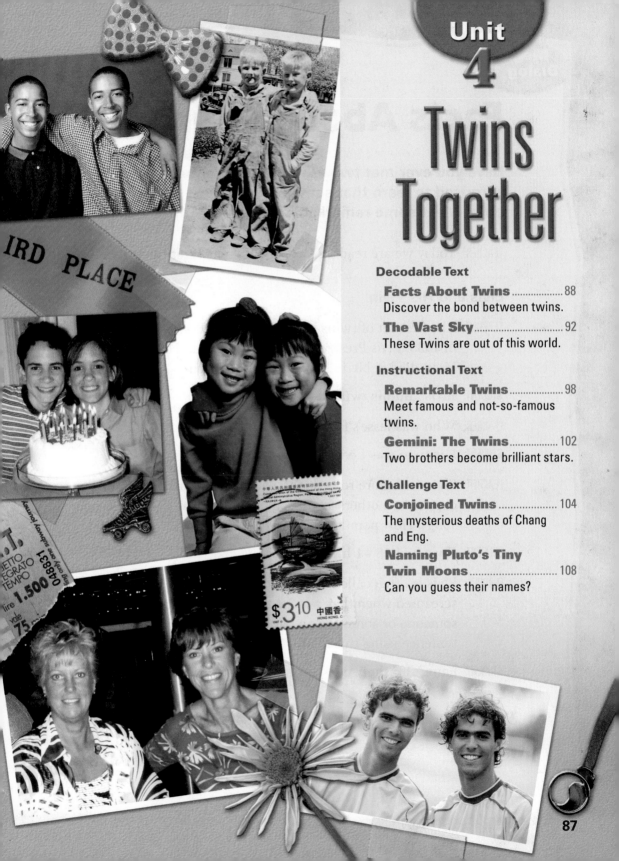

Twins Together

Facts About Twins

Have you ever met twins? Have you ever been surprised to learn that someone you knew had a twin? Meet some remarkable twins.

TEACHER: Today we are reading facts about some interesting twins.

Elvis and His Twin

TEACHER: The first set of twins is Elvis and Jesse Presley. They were born in 1935. Elvis Presley was a famous singer. His twin brother, Jesse, died at birth. When were they born?

STUDENT: Elvis and his twin were born in 1935.

TEACHER: Who was Jesse's famous twin?

STUDENT: His twin was Elvis.

TEACHER: Elvis sold more records than anyone. Recordings that sell more copies than others are called hits. Elvis had 18 number one songs. How popular was Elvis?

STUDENT: Elvis had 18 #1 hits.

TEACHER: Elvis is often called the "King of Rock and Roll." Teenage girls screamed when they watched him sing. An idiom for liking someone or something a lot is to "flip your lid." Paraphrase this sentence using this idiom: "Fans go crazy for Elvis."

STUDENT: Fans "flip their lids" for him.

TEACHER: Elvis also made many movies in which his singing was a prominent feature. What else did Elvis do besides make records?

STUDENT: Elvis was in hit films.

TEACHER: In Elvis' day, a slang word for a home was a "pad." Elvis' home as an adult was in Memphis. He named his home Graceland. Use slang to paraphrase.

STUDENT: His pad was Graceland.

TEACHER: Elvis was nominated for a Grammy 14 times.

STUDENT: What did Elvis win?

TEACHER: During his career, Elvis won three Grammies for his music.

TEACHER: When Elvis died, he was buried at his home in Memphis. He was buried beside his twin, Jesse. Where are these twins buried?

STUDENT: Elvis and his twin are at Graceland.

TEACHER: Since his death, thousands of people visit Graceland every year to honor "the King." What can you say about Elvis?

STUDENT: Elvis is famous.
Ask a fan if he lives!

The Baker Twins

TEACHER: The first set of twins we read about were men. The next set of twins are women. Their names are Kari and Kim Baker. Who is Kari?

STUDENT: She is Kim's twin.

TEACHER: Where do the twins live?

STUDENT: Kari and Kim Baker live in a small town in a northern state called Montana.

TEACHER: Kari and Kim have a ranch in Montana. They raise horses. They have lots of dogs and cats and even a pet pig. Tell me about some of their animals.

STUDENT: They have a pack of pets. The twins have cats, horses, and a pig!

TEACHER: These two twins are inseparable. That means they can't imagine being apart. They have always lived together. Paraphrase how the twins seem to be.

STUDENT: The twins are connected.

TEACHER: They stay in shape with their work at the ranch. How do the twins stay in shape? I'll say the sentence using "Kari," then you say it using "Kim": "Kari has tasks."

STUDENT: Kim has tasks.

TEACHER: Paraphrase: "The twins are in shape."

STUDENT: The twins are fit.

TEACHER: I'd like you to paraphrase again: "Kim and Kari are best friends."

STUDENT: The twins admit they are pals.

TEACHER: When the horses' hooves or manes need to be trimmed, Kari and Kim work together. What chore do the twins do together?

STUDENT: **The twins trim the horses.**

TEACHER: Since they live up north, they have to cut firewood. Another word for "cut" is "split." Paraphrase this sentence: "Both Kari and Kim cut firewood."

STUDENT: **The twins split wood.**

TEACHER: Kari and Kim live up north. They use the firewood to keep warm. Other words that mean "cold" are "crisp" and "brisk." Use these words to describe how the air feels when you need a fire.

STUDENT: **It is crisp and brisk.**

TEACHER: The sisters disagree on one thing. Kari says their horses can't tell them apart. Kim says they can. Did Kim say the horses can or cannot tell which twin is which?

STUDENT: **Kim said they can.**

TEACHER: Let's summarize. While these twins are not famous on a grand scale, they are famous in Libby, Montana! They have their animals to make their lives feel complete. Most importantly, they have each other. Say these sentences using the other twin's name: "Kari's twin is a big fan of Kari." "Kari is a big fan of her twin."

STUDENT: **Kim's twin is a big fan of Kim. Kim is a big fan of her twin.**

TEACHER: We've read about some remarkable twins. We met a rock and roll star and Montana ranchers! What is this selection's title?

STUDENT: **It is "Facts About Twins."**

The Vast Sky

**Twins come in all shapes and sizes. Sometimes
they appear in the most unexpected places.**

These twins are found in the sky.

TEACHER: These twins are celestial. Celestial means that they are found in
the sky as opposed to on Earth. Where are these twins found?

STUDENT: The twins are in the vast sky.

TEACHER: The celestial twins are located in the constellation Gemini.
What kind of stars does the constellation Gemini contain?

STUDENT: It has twins.

TEACHER: Constellations are manmade, artificial ways to recognize
clusters of stars in the sky. Designs have been drawn around
these groups of stars and given names. The lines don't exist. In
other words, they are not real. We have to imagine the lines and
create a picture of the real thing in our minds. We use the word
"abstract" when we try to imagine real objects when they don't
exist. We use the word "concrete" for objects that are real. Is a
constellation concrete or abstract?

STUDENT: It is abstract.

TEACHER: What about a star?

STUDENT: Is it abstract?

TEACHER: No, a star is real. It is concrete, but the constellation is abstract.
Let's talk about the designs that have been drawn around these
star patterns and then given names. We've already learned that

This 17th century Persian illustration shows the constellation Gemini.

the twin stars are in Gemini. Everyone on Earth sees these constellations. However, people in different cultures have seen the same constellation as different things.

STUDENT: **What did they see?**

TEACHER: The Arabic culture named it "twin peacocks." The Egyptians called the constellation the "twin plants." What was it called by the Egyptians?

STUDENT: **Its name was the twin plants.**

TEACHER: In the Hindu population, this same constellation was known by yet another name. What did they name it?

STUDENT: **The Hindus called it the "twin gods."**

TEACHER: There are many other named constellations. You have probably heard of some. The zodiac names are examples of some of these constellations. A set of imaginary lines has been drawn around the stars of Gemini. These lines come together to represent a pair of twins. Thus, Gemini is called the Twins. Paraphrase this sentence.

STUDENT: **It stands for the Twins.**

TEACHER: Each zodiac symbol represents a set time period on our calendar. Gemini is associated with late May and June. Aries is another zodiac symbol, which is associated with late March and April. The animal symbol for Aries is the Ram. Paraphrase this sentence.

STUDENT: It stands for the Ram.

TEACHER: Cancer the Crab is linked to the summer months of June and July. What does Cancer stand for?

STUDENT: It stands for the Crab.

TEACHER: People have been studying the stars for thousands of years. They began looking at the stars to study the passage of time. When did people start wondering about the stars?

STUDENT: It was in the past.

TEACHER: Let's talk about how ancient people used the stars. One way they used the stars was to navigate or steer their ships. They used them to plan their trips. How did ancient sailors use the stars?

STUDENT: They used them to plan trips.

TEACHER: To help them navigate across the oceans, they made maps of the stars. I'll say a sentence in past tense. You change it to present tense: "The sailors mapped the stars."

STUDENT: They map the stars.

TEACHER: Farmers needed to know when to plant different crops during the year.

STUDENT: When did they plant?

TEACHER: Farmers planted their crops according to the stars. The positions of the constellations in the night sky told them it was time to plant. Sometimes, farmers planted seeds. Other times, they set out sprigs, or small plants. What can a man plant in his fields instead of seeds?

STUDENT: A man can plant sprigs.

TEACHER: Tell me two ways people used stars in the past.

STUDENT: In the past, they were used to plan trips and to plant sprigs.

TEACHER: People everywhere have used the abstract concept of constellations to help them break the sky into segments or bits. By dividing the sky into segments or constellations, people can more easily remember the location and name of the countless stars in the sky. Why did people create the concept of constellations?

STUDENT: It splits the sky in segments.

TEACHER: An astronomer's job is to search, or scan, the heavens for stars and planets. Tell me the first part of his job.

STUDENT: His task is to scan the sky.

TEACHER: He names his discoveries and shares them with other scientists. Tell me another part of an astronomer's job.

STUDENT: His task is to name the stars.

TEACHER: Stars seem to move across the sky. They really don't move, but the Earth does. It spins on its axis. The Earth is also at an angle, or tilt. The Earth's rotation makes the stars appear to move. What does the Earth do to make the constellations appear to move in the sky?

STUDENT: It tilts and spins.

TEACHER: Although the stars do not move, other objects in the sky do move. Satellites travel across the sky and are visible at night. When a satellite orbits in the night sky, it may be barely visible. How could we describe its brightness?

STUDENT: In the vast sky, it is dim.

TEACHER: Satellites are used to send information through space from one place on Earth to another. Use synonyms to replace "send" with "transmit" and "information" with "facts": A satellite is used to send information.

STUDENT: It is used to transmit facts.

TEACHER: It's time to review some of the facts from this selection. The constellation Gemini has bright twin stars. What is significant about the constellation Gemini?

STUDENT: It has twin stars, and these stars are bright.

TEACHER: Twelve constellations have been linked to our calendar. These are called the signs of the zodiac. We hit on three of the zodiac signs in this selection. What are they?

STUDENT: We hit on the Twins, the Ram, and the Crab.

TEACHER: Right. Gemini represents the Twins. Aries stands for the Ram. The Crab represents Cancer. While constellations appear to move across the sky, really the Earth's rotation causes this illusion. What does the Earth do to make the stars seem to drift?

STUDENT: It tilts and spins.

TEACHER: Finally, we talked about other things we see in the night sky, like satellites. We learned they help us communicate by sending information. What does a satellite do?

STUDENT: It transmits facts.

TEACHER: What is the title of this selection?

STUDENT: It is "The Vast Sky."

Remarkable Twins

Have you ever thought of what it would be like to be a twin? Here are the stories of three sets of twins. These stories tell about the special bond between twins. Read about them and learn what it is like to be a twin.

Elvis and Jesse Presley

5   Elvis Presley was born in 1935 in Mississippi. He was the King of Rock and Roll. Everyone knows Elvis. But what does anyone know about Jesse? Do you know who he was? Jesse was Elvis' brother, and he was Elvis' twin. Jesse died at birth.

10   Elvis went on to be a star. For the Christmas of 1946, Elvis wanted a bike. His parents couldn't afford

one, so instead they gave him a guitar.
It cost $12.95. That was the beginning
of his musical career. Elvis made
15 history. He sold more records than
anyone. He had 18 number one songs.
Elvis also had 14 Grammy **nominations**,
and he won three Grammy awards.

Elvis was **remarkable**. At times, he
20 spoke of his twin, even though he never
knew him. Elvis always felt connected to
Jesse. Elvis died in 1977 at Graceland,
his home in Memphis. Elvis and Jesse
are buried together there in the garden.
25 They were born together. In the end,
they are together again.

Kim and Kari Baker

There are 2,600 people who live in
Libby, Montana. Libby has a drive-in and two **llama**
farms. It also has a special set of twins, Kim and Kari
30 Baker. The Bakers are ranchers and photographers.

These twins were born in Montana. They have
been riding horses since they were nine years old. They
have always loved horses and all kinds of animals. For
years, they showed horses in competitions and won
35 many awards. Now, they work on their ranch. They
also take photos and write articles about horses.

Kim and Kari have always been close. They have
lots of chores to do around the ranch. They take turns
feeding the horses. They both cut firewood. (They need
40 a big supply of firewood for the winter.) When it's time
to trim horses' hooves, Kari trims the right side and
Kim trims the left.

Can their horses tell them apart? Kari says they
can't, but Kim thinks they can. "Yes, the horses *can*
45 tell us apart. They know us as individuals. Animals are
more **aware** than people."

nominations
names of people to
be picked for a job
or award

remarkable
worth noticing;
special or
uncommon

llama
a long-haired
animal related to
the camel

aware
watchful of or
knowing about

Scott Kelly

Mark Kelly

Mark and Scott Kelly

Are there twins who have flown into space?
Mark and Scott Kelly have. They are twins who grew
up in New Jersey. In 1996, they both applied to be
50 **astronauts**. Only 35 candidates were selected out of
3,500 who applied. NASA selected both of the Kelly
twins. What is the chance of *both* being selected? The
Kellys became the first twins to fly in space. In 1999,
Scott went up. He became the first twin to fly in space.
55 He flew on the space shuttle *Discovery* and worked on
the Hubble Space Telescope.

Two years later, Mark was assigned to a mission. He
flew in the space shuttle *Endeavour*.

What else do the Kellys have in common? Both
60 are space shuttle pilots. Both are test pilots. Both are
combat pilots and Navy lieutenant commanders. Both
are engineers. Both are married, and their daughters
are the same age. Their daughters have even played on
the same soccer team!
65 In 2003, the space shuttle *Columbia* met with
tragedy, but Mark and Scott knew that someday they
would fly again. In 2006, Mark traveled aboard the
space shuttle *Discovery* to the International Space
Station. Next, it's Scott's turn.

astronauts
people trained for
space flight

combat
having to do with a
fight or battle

Adapted with permission from
"Twin Portraits" and "Twinnacle of Success"
by Craig Sanders, Twinstuff.com

Answer It
Say the answer in a complete sentence.

1. When did Elvis get a guitar?
2. What did Kim and Kari Baker do on their ranch?
3. When did NASA select both Kellys?
4. When did Scott become the first twin to fly in space?
5. Who flew the *Endeavour* space shuttle?

Gemini: The Twins

Castor   Pollux

On a dark night, turn your eyes up to the dark sky. Look for the **constellation** Gemini. It has two very bright **stars** called the Twins. People have known about them for thousands of years. They have been in
5 the sky as long as anyone can remember.

Ancient people invented stories about these two stars. The Greeks said they were the sons of the Greek god Zeus and the woman Leda. What did others call these two stars? Arabs called them twin peacocks. The
10 Egyptians called them twin plants. Hindus called them twin gods.

What are constellations?

What are constellations? They are patterns of stars that people see in the sky. These star patterns were invented by people fascinated with the stars. Ancient
15 **poets** made up stories about them. How long have we

constellation
a group of stars that form a shape

stars
large objects in space that look like points of light in the night sky

poets
writers of verse

102 Unit 4 • Twins Together

been seeing patterns in the night sky? We have done it for at least 6,000 years.

Why did the idea of constellations begin?

Why were star groups made up? There are so many stars! How could we remember them all? We could
20 put them in groups! The groups break the sky into parts. They help us remember which stars are which. How many can we see? On a dark night, we see 1,000 to 1,500 stars. Where can we see the Twins? We can see them in the northern hemisphere in November
25 through April. We can see them in the southern hemisphere in December through March.

The ancient Greek story of Gemini

The ancient Greeks said that Zeus and Leda had twin sons. Their names were Castor and Pollux. They were devoted and loving brothers. They looked alike.
30 But they were not alike. Castor was **mortal** like his mother. He became a horseman. Pollux was **immortal** like his father. He became a boxer. Both became expert soldiers. Castor was killed in battle. Pollux could not bear to be without his twin. Pollux asked his father,
35 Zeus, for help. He asked for Castor to come back to life. Zeus let them be together side by side forever. They are the Twins that shine brightly in the sky. They are the two **brilliant** stars in Gemini.

mortal
something or someone that will die someday

immortal
something or someone that will never die

brilliant
very bright; giving off lots of light

Answer It
Say the answer in a complete sentence.

1. What is Gemini?
2. Who told stories about constellations?
3. When is Gemini seen in the northern hemisphere?
4. When is Gemini seen in the southern hemisphere?
5. Who made Castor and Pollux into brilliant stars?

Conjoined Twins

Chang and Eng

Conjoined twins Chang and Eng lived 63 years of celebrity, tragedy, and normalcy. And when they died, they left an amazing but unanswered question.

Brothers Chang and Eng achieved world
5 recognition because they were inseparable, literally. They were the first widely known conjoined twins. They were born with a thick band of tissue connecting their chests.

Born in Siam (now Thailand), Chang and Eng
10 inspired the name "Siamese twins." Doctors debated separating them, but were not sure if the twins would survive the surgery.

Still, the twins learned to run, jump, and swim and lead relatively normal lives. Their father died when
15 they were young. As teenagers, they did chores and helped support the family by gathering and selling duck eggs in their small village.

About this time, Chang and Eng were discovered by Robert Hunter, a British **merchant**, who portrayed
20 himself as a savior and benefactor. Yet, he was a wolf in sheep's clothing. He won their mother as an ally with talk of wealth and fame for the twins. Several years passed before the king let them leave Siam. Their

merchant
a person who buys and sells things for a living

*Chang and Eng Bunker
were born in Siam.*

mother had sold the boys to Hunter for $3,000. The
25 agreement would end in 2½ years, and their mother
received only $500.

Hunter and his partner managed the twins.
Working constantly, the twins were exhibited in
theaters and concert halls. The twins toured America
30 and England. Admission was about 50 cents. The
managers pushed the twins to the point of exhaustion.

Then at 21, Chang and Eng became independent.
They had been Siamese boys with no knowledge of the

"Conjoined twins" is the correct term for twins who are physically joined. The term "Siamese twins" is derogatory.

telepathic
communicating through means other than senses

prefer
to choose a more desirable option

outside world. Now, they were worldly men who were
35 drawn to learning and culture.

Many newspaper articles described the twins. Chang was an inch shorter than his brother. But he made up for it in temper; Chang was thought to be dominant. He was mentally faster, but faster to anger.
40 Eng was taciturn, a man of few words. Eng had wider interests than Chang. These characteristics hardened in their later lives.

Despite minor differences, the twins continued to amaze people. Their relationship seemed good. With few
45 exceptions, they acted as one. They shared tastes and opinions. Some imagined that they were **telepathic**. After all, the two rarely spoke to each other!

After becoming naturalized U.S. citizens, they chose to join the mainstream of American life. They
50 changed their last name to Bunker, married sisters, and became farmers.

At several points in their lives, Chang and Eng were tempted to risk a separation surgery. But each time, they were convinced by doctors or relatives that the
55 procedure was too perilous. Ugly altercations marred the twins' later lives. During one, Chang threatened Eng with a knife. Furious, the two went to their family doctor. They demanded immediate separation. Calmly, the surgeon laid out his instruments. He turned to
60 them and asked, "Which would you **prefer**? Shall I sever the flesh that connects you? Or shall I cut off your heads? One will produce the same result as the other." The second option was enough to change the twins' minds.

65 Their doctor made a promise to them that he would perform the operation immediately upon the demise of either one of the brothers. Sadly, he was not present when Chang died.

Eng and Chang Bunker died on a cold January
70 night in 1874. They left the world as they entered it 63 years before—together. Had Chang's death—he

perished first—been a catalyst for Eng's? And would that mean, as had doctors predicted, each could not exist without the other?

75   But there were many complicating factors. Chang had suffered a stroke four years before. His health had become **frail**. He was also a heavy drinker. He had **bronchitis**. Recently, he had been hurt in a **carriage** accident. Eng, on the other hand, had been in good
80 health, unaffected by his brother's poor health.

        After their deaths, doctors disagreed. A blood clot had ended Chang's life. Some doctors thought that Eng had died of shock. They said Eng was literally scared to death. Others believed that the band that connected
85 the twins was a lifeline and ultimately passed death from one to the other. They found a blood clot in Chang's brain. Eng's death remains a mystery.

        In 1897, the American Medical Association determined that if the twins had survived until the late
90 1890s, recent advances in surgical medicine, including antiseptics, would have made it possible for them to be separated.

Adapted with permission from
"A Hyphenated Life" by Page Chichester

> **frail**
> weak, sickly

> **bronchitis**
> an infection of the tubes that lead to the lungs

> **carriage**
> a horse-drawn vehicle with wheels

Think About It

1. Where were Chang and Eng joined?

2. Chang and Eng were identical twins. They looked alike. In what ways were they different?

3. At age 63, Chang died of a blood clot. What was the cause of Eng's death?

4. When Chang and Eng learned that the surgery to separate them might end their lives, they quickly reconsidered. Do you think their decision improved their relationship? Why or why not?

5. Some people mistreat people who are different. Why do you think they do this? If you could, what would you say to these people?

6. Suppose you were conjoined to a twin, and you could not be separated. How would life be more difficult for you? Think of at least six things that would be very difficult.

NAMING PLUTO'S TINY TWIN MOONS

June 22, 2006—Two tiny twin moons discovered
by the Hubble Space Telescope in 2005 have been
officially named Nix and Hydra. Their names were
approved last week by the International Astronomical
5 Union (IAU). The IAU is the recognized group that
approves the names of newly discovered space objects.

Why were such unusual names chosen? Pluto and
its bigger moon, Charon, which was discovered in
1978, are named after characters in Greek mythology.
10 In these myths, Pluto was the lord of the underworld.
Charon steered the boat that brought souls across the
river Styx to Pluto.

Andrew Steffl helped name the tiny moons. He
is with the Southwest Research Institute in Boulder,
15 Colorado. He thought hard to come up with the perfect
names for these twins.

"I was having trouble sleeping one night. So I went
and did a Web search for things related to Pluto and
Charon," Steffl said.

Nix
the goddess of the night and mother of Charon

Hydra
the mythological nine-headed beast
that guarded the entrance to Pluto's realm

Andrew Steffl is one of the astronomers credited with
discovering the moons.

20   Steffl talked with his co-discoverers and came
up with a list of **proposed** names. They sent these
names to the IAU. At the top of the list was Nix. Nix
(or Nyx) was the goddess of the night and the mother
of Charon. Another name was Hydra. Hydra was a
25 serpent with nine heads. Hydra guarded the entrance
to Pluto's underworld.

    Although we know that Nix and Hydra orbit Pluto,
we don't know too much more about them. They
are 5,000 times fainter than Pluto. Their estimated
30 diameters are between 40 and 125 miles. Charon, for
comparison, is about 730 miles wide. Pluto is about
1,410 miles in diameter.

    Some astronomers have a **theory** that Pluto's
moons were formed together. They think this because
35 the twin moons' rotations are similar to Charon's.

    Like Earth's moon, Pluto's moons may have been
formed when an asteroid or comet smashed into Pluto.
This would have happened a long time ago when Pluto
was forming.

proposed
suggested

theory
idea or explanation
not proven
scientifically

Pluto
Nix
Charon
Hydra

Hubble Space Telescope Photo

gravity

natural pull between celestial bodies

scenario

an outline of expected events

40   Another theory is that the tiny moons were captured by Pluto's **gravity** . They perhaps came from the Kuiper Belt. This region beyond Neptune is filled with small orbiting space objects.

    The moons were discovered last year in images
45 taken by the Hubble. Steffl spent days studying the pictures. "It was really a what-if **scenario** ," he said.

    To help his search, he created a four-frame movie from the Hubble images. He put random artificial moons in them. When he saw the real moons, he didn't
50 believe it at first.

    "I put the artificial moons in, but I didn't know where they were," he said. "When I found the real moons, I assumed they were a part of the program. Then, when I realized what they were, I just about fell
55 off my chair."

    Steffl didn't know that there were two other scientists looking for additional moons around Pluto too. They ended up making the same discovery. One was Max Mutchler at the Space Telescope Science
60 Institute in Baltimore, Maryland. The other was Hal Weaver, with the Johns Hopkins University Applied Physics Laboratory in Laurel, Maryland.

    The discovery makes Pluto the first object in the Kuiper Belt with more than one moon. Could Pluto
65 have even more moons? A second study is planned with the Hubble next year. Also, a satellite is on its way to Pluto for a close-up look in 2015.

An Eye on the Stars—The Hubble

Every 97 minutes, the Hubble orbits the Earth. It sends back images of planets, solar systems, and galaxies. Like other telescopes, the Hubble works by collecting more light than the human eye can see on its own. On Earth, telescopes must capture light from distant objects through the shifting air of the Earth's atmosphere. This **distortion** of the atmosphere makes stars appear to twinkle in the sky. The Hubble orbits 353 miles above the atmosphere to give us a clear view of enormous galaxies and small heavenly bodies like the tiny twin moons. Launched in 1990, the Hubble will be replaced by a more powerful space telescope in 2013.

distortion
imperfect view

What's in a Name?—The IAU

If you discovered a planet, moon, or star, could you name it after your best friend, your favorite teacher, or your dog? Without the approval of the International Astronomical Union (IAU), you wouldn't have a chance. The IAU consists of professional astronomers from all over the world. They promote the science of astronomy. They give the final approval to the names of space objects. The IAU approved the names for Pluto's twin moons.

Pluto loses planet statu[s]
Pluto a "dwarf planet" instead.

After years of debate, Pluto lost its status as a[n]
planet of our solar system in August 2006. IA[U]
omers from around the world voted in favor o[f]
Pluto a "dwarf planet" instead. The discovery
Pluto sits within the Kuiper Belt is part of the
that Pluto's planet status was changed. The ei[ght]
planets, including Earth, seem to have broa[d]
space ar... ...rbits. Pluto an[d] [i]ts mo[o]

Pluto—The Unplanet

After years of **debate**, Pluto lost its status as an official planet of our solar system in August 2006. IAU astronomers from around the world voted in favor of calling Pluto a "dwarf planet" instead. The discovery that Pluto sits within the Kuiper Belt is part of the reason that Pluto's planet status was changed. The eight large planets, including Earth, seem to have broad bands of space around their orbits. Pluto and its moons orbit with many objects of similar size. These can also be considered "dwarf planets."

debate

formal discussion or argument

Think About It

1. When and how were the two tiny moons of Pluto discovered?

2. Why do you think the newly discovered twin moons were named Nix and Hydra?

3. Astronomers think there are two possible ways in which Pluto's moons were formed. Describe these two theories.

4. What advantage does the Hubble Space Telescope have over Earth-based telescopes?

5. An astronomer is a specially trained physicist who studies objects in outer space beyond the Earth's atmosphere. Would you like to be an astronomer? Why or why not?

Unit
5

Jazz It Up

What Is Jazz?

Relax, kick back, and discover jazz. Jazz reminds us of our past, and jazz still lives today.

TEACHER: Music is a language of its own. It has a written code and recognized, meaningful symbols. Jazz is a kind of music. What is jazz?

STUDENT: Jazz is a kind of music.

TEACHER: Jazz is a type or kind of music. There are many kinds of music. You might be more familiar with rock or rap. What are jazz, rock, and rap?

STUDENT: Jazz, rock, and rap are kinds of music.

TEACHER: Many styles of music have their roots in classical music. Composers of classical music wrote very specific note sequences for musicians to play. Jazz differs from classical music. The difference has to do with how the musician uses written music. What is the difference?

STUDENT: Musicians of classical music stick to the music. Jazz musicians do not. They jam.

TEACHER: When jazz musicians play their songs, they often add notes that are not written down. This is called improvising or "jamming." A "jam session" is where musicians create new music or add to existing music as they play. How do jazz musicians make their music different?

STUDENT: Jazz bands add notes that are not in the music. The notes they add can have a fantastic impact!

TEACHER: Some people like classical music for its style. Some people criticize it because it is rigid. What do critics of classical music think of jazz?

STUDENT: The critics think that jazz is fantastic. They do not think it is rigid.

TEACHER: Over time, classical music has had an influence on current styles of music. What types of music do you think have been influenced by classical music?

STUDENT: Classical music has had an impact on rock, rap, and hip-hop.

TEACHER: In addition to classical music, several other kinds of traditional music have developed to reflect people's daily lives. Several of these styles of music formed the foundation for jazz. Work songs, church music, ballads, ragtime, and the blues are ingredients of jazz. What was the foundation of jazz?

STUDENT: Music from the past impacted jazz.

TEACHER: Jazz is an American music form that has evolved from many different kinds of music. Work songs were a natural development. This type of music made long days of working on the railroads or tending crops in the fields pass a little more rapidly. With hammers or hoes in hand, workers would coordinate their movements to a steady beat. What did jazz do for the workers?

STUDENT: Music acted as a prompt to work together. They did tasks to the music. It made the day pass fast.

TEACHER: Church music also influenced jazz. African Americans made new kinds of church music. They rewrote the old songs and gave them new words, a new beat, and a new tune. This music played a part in jazz.

STUDENT: This music had an impact too.

TEACHER: In ballads, music was simply the format for storytelling. While many ballads were based on real people and real events, details were added that were not necessarily true. What type of music tells a story?

STUDENT: Ballads do.

TEACHER: Ragtime music was also popular in the past. It was a lively and loud form of music. Pianos were an essential part of ragtime music. People liked dancing to ragtime.

STUDENT: Ragtime music is fast and brisk. Ragtime is a part of jazz.

TEACHER: The "blues" also contributed to jazz in America. Blues reflected the darker side of life. These performers knew many hardships and put those feelings into their music. What ingredient do you think the blues contribute to the sound of jazz?

STUDENT: This strand of jazz adds a sad sound. Bands ad-lib to make this kind of music.

TEACHER: Blues musicians often add notes that are not written down. This type of music is improvised, or ad-libbed. What makes the blues different from classical music?

STUDENT: Bands ad-lib in this strand of jazz. They kick back and jam to play the blues. Blues, ballads, and ragtime are strands of jazz.

TEACHER: The mixture of musical elements created jazz. Jazz was extremely popular in the 1920s. This period was known as the Jazz Age. People flocked to hear jazz played. They listened and danced to the music.

STUDENT: Jazz was a hit with fans.

TEACHER: Jazz music has inspired artists to try to capture the mood and feeling of the music. Sometimes, in their work it's easy to see the performers and their audience. When an artist paints a jazz concert, what can they capture on their canvas?

STUDENT: The band and fans are in the picture.

TEACHER: It isn't as easy to "see" the music. Some artists create bold, colorful lines to help us imagine the music and the mood. The types of lines and colors help capture the music on canvas. Artists try to create visual images to match the music.

STUDENT: A picture of jazz is vivid and abstract.

TEACHER: In the early days of photography, bands being photographed had to sit perfectly still for at least a minute. With faster film, such posing for a picture was no longer necessary. The photographs could be as spontaneous and candid as the music. What is it like when photographers can use fast film and a portable flash to capture a jazz performance?

STUDENT: The film is fast. The jazz band jams. The pictures are candid.

TEACHER: Jazz is truly an American music form. It has its roots in the past, yet it has endured. Jazz continues to be popular today.

STUDENT: The past lives in jazz. Jazz is still a hit. It is not a fad.

Jazz: The Recipe

How did jazz begin? There was a " **recipe** " that had many different ingredients. There were different groups of people, including Africans and Europeans. There were different kinds of music, including the
5 blues and ragtime. All of these combined to make America's own music, **jazz**. Here are some of the important ingredients.

Workers sang songs as they worked together. They sang in fields and on ships. They sang while working
10 on the railroads. The **work song** was an important part of their day. With hammers or hoes in their hands, they worked to a steady beat. The songs made life a little easier. There were many kinds of work songs, and these songs played a part in jazz.
15 **Church music** was important to jazz. African Americans made new kinds of church music. They

formed their own churches and rewrote the old songs. They changed the words, the beat, and the tune. They used the African " **call and response** " when they sang. 20 This music played a part in jazz.

Music of white Americans added to jazz. The Scotch-Irish had **ballads**. Ballads often tell stories of heroes and their bravery, and these stories are often sad. The song is usually simple. In a ballad, the story is 25 often more important than the music. Ballads played a part in jazz.

In early America, ballroom **dance music** was popular. In the South, **plantations** held dances. They were big social events. There was a demand for 30 musicians to play at the dances. Many slaves learned how to play fiddles and flutes. African Americans invented the banjo and played it too. Black musicians learned the dance songs and changed them. African and European music combined. Dance music played a 35 part in jazz.

During the 1800s, a new kind of music called **ragtime** was born. It was loud and fun. Musicians pounded on their pianos. They played in dance halls. The tunes were lively, and the rhythm was catchy. 40 Everybody loved ragtime. It had a strong, irregular beat that was surprising. Ragtime played a part in jazz.

When were the **blues** first played? They were played sometime in the late 1800s. The slaves were free, but life was still hard. People were sad and frustrated. They 45 expressed their feelings in music. They called it the blues. Today, people still sing the blues when they're sad. The blues played a part in jazz.

The jazz recipe came together in **New Orleans** ! By 1890, New Orleans was one of America's most 50 musical cities. It had **opera** houses and concert halls. It had dance ballrooms and street parades. It had the **Mardi Gras** ! Many different people lived there. There were Africans and Native Americans. There were

call and response
a singing or speaking style where one person or group sings or says something and another group answers by singing or saying something

plantations
large farms or areas of land

New Orleans
a city in southeastern Louisiana

opera
a play set to music

Mardi Gras
a holiday in New Orleans with parades and carnivals

French and Spanish. There were people from many
55 places and cultures. Together, they created America's
own music, jazz.

Adapted from *Cobblestone*, "Jazz Ingredients"
by Heather Mitchell Amey, © by Carus Publishing Company.
Reproduced with permission.

Answer It
Say the answer in a complete sentence.

1. Where did people sing work songs?
2. What did African Americans do to change church music?
3. What stories do ballads tell?
4. Why were freed slaves singing the blues?
5. Where did all the different music come together?

Photograph ©2004 Museum of Fine Arts, Boston

LOOKING AT JAZZ

Everyone knows that we can *listen* to jazz, but do you know that we can *see* it as well? From the beginning of jazz, artists and photographers have tried to capture its spirit in art. Some artists show musicians
5 performing. Others show people dancing to the music. Others create abstract pictures that try to capture the **mood** and the feeling of jazz.

mood
the feeling created by something

The 1920s were called the Jazz Age. Jazz was so popular it was like rock today. In the 1920s, there was a
10 new spirit. Young people loved jazz. It made them feel alive and free. They wanted to have fun. Flappers were young women with short hair and short skirts. They

shocked some old folks. Flappers loved dancing to jazz.
They did the Charleston, the most popular jazz dance.

15   Artists loved to paint the flappers dancing. Artists
sketched pictures of young people crowding the jazz
clubs to dance. They didn't always draw or paint
exactly what they saw. They would use different types
of lines and **bold** colors to create moods. Curved lines
20 are restful. Zigzag lines are nervous. Black is powerful.
Red is exciting. Artists changed the scene to capture
the feeling of excitement when people were dancing.
They painted jazz.

    Music **inspires** art. You can see that in the
25 paintings. They *look* like jazz. With their wild colors
and crazy lines, they have a **rhythm**. They look like
the music.

bold
easily seen, flashy

inspires
causes a person to
do something

rhythm
a regular pattern,
such as beats in
music

abstraction
art that doesn't
look like a real
object

Photograph ©2004 Museum of Fine Arts, Boston

*Hot Still Scape With Six Colors—
Seventh Avenue Style*

*Hot Still Scape
With Six Colors—
Seventh Avenue
Style* is a jazzy
title.

It is an
abstraction by
Stuart Davis, an
American artist.
Stuart often said
that the spirit of
jazz inspired all
of his art.

    Many photographers captured jazz too. Some of
the first photographs of jazz musicians were made by
30 an African American photographer, Arthur Bedou,
who lived in New Orleans. By the 1940s, photography
had improved. Film was faster, and the flash became
portable. Photographers could capture the moment at

jazz shows. They could find the right angle and snap
35 the picture quickly.

Over the years, artists and photographers have tried
many ways to capture the look and feel of jazz. The
paintings and the photographs are like the music—
strong, alive, and free. They are **distinct** . They *are* jazz!

Adapted from *Cobblestone*, "Looking at Jazz" by Marc H. Miller,
© by Carus Publishing Company. Reproduced with permission.

distinct
clearly different
from others; worth
noticing

Lisette Model's
photograph of Louis
Armstrong performing
at the Newport Jazz
Festival looks simple.
But it was the result
of hard work. It took
careful calculation and
quick reflexes.

©The Lisette Model Foundation, Inc. (1983). Used by permission/Art Resource, NY

Louis Armstrong performs at the Newport Jazz Festival. Photographed by Lisette Model.

Answer It
Say the answer in a complete sentence.

1. What do pictures of jazz show?

2. When was the Jazz Age?

3. Why did young people like jazz during the Jazz Age?

4. Why did artists use different lines and bold colors?

5. Why were photographers finally able to take pictures at jazz shows?

Growing Up With Jazz

"When I was a kid, I would rather do without food than without music." Who said that? The person who dominated the jazz world for half a century. Louis Armstrong. Satchmo. The most beloved jazzman who
5 ever lived.

Louis Armstrong was the revered statesman of jazz because he altered the landscape of American music. Benefiting from the example of other musicians and the encouragement of his wife, he emerged victorious
10 despite hardship.

On August 4, 1901, Louis was born in New Orleans. There, people said that Louis and jazz were born together. Louis said it himself. "Jazz and I grew up

side by side." He lived in a home without electricity or
15 plumbing. Louis' father left the family when Louis was
a baby, and times were hard.

By the fifth grade, Louis left school. Looking for
ways to earn money, he hit the streets and peddled
newspapers and delivered buckets of coal from a mule-
20 drawn wagon. With his earnings, his mother could
buy food and cook. Louis loved the red beans and rice
the people of New Orleans still love today. Most of
all, Louis loved listening to the bands that played in
parades and funerals. Recalling those days, Armstrong
25 later commented, "Even the pie man used to play
something on the **bugle** . The waffle man rang a big
triangle. The junk man had one of them long tin horns.
In New Orleans, there was always something that was
nice, and always with music." Louis himself sang on
30 street corners with a group of friends. He was with
friends when he got into bad trouble.

It was New Year's Eve. Louis was about 11 years old.
He wanted to have some fun and impress his friends.
From a street corner, he fired a pistol he had taken
35 from his stepfather. He was arrested and sent to the
Colored **Waifs**' Home, a reform school. Amazingly,
Louis "took to it." For the first time, he had regular
meals and clean clothes. Best of all, the home had a
marching band. Louis learned to play the trumpet!
40 Within a year, he proudly led the band through his old
neighborhood.

When he got out, Louis spent his days hauling coal.
He spent his nights in the honky-tonks, begging for
a chance to sit in with a band. Years passed before he
45 snagged a job in a dance hall.

In 1922, Armstrong received a **telegram** from
Chicago ordering him to "come immediately. I have
a job for you in my band." It was from his old friend
and mentor, the famous "King" Oliver. With a few
50 dollars in his pocket, his horn, and a fish sandwich,
he took the train to Chicago. In Chicago, Armstrong

bugle
a trumpet-shaped
horn without keys

waifs
abandoned
children; orphans

telegram
a message sent
by a code-making
machine

met Lillian Hardin, the young pianist in King Oliver's band. She and Armstrong were married in 1924, with Lil determined to make him "believe in himself" and

55 strike out on his own.

With Lil's encouragement, his career took off. He made some of his most famous records during the 1920s and became the idol of jazz musicians. He played in legendary bands in Chicago and New York. He

60 toured Europe, where, much to his surprise, his records were already famous.

Increasingly, Louis became a show business entertainer. He appeared on **Broadway**, and he was featured on radio programs and in the movies.

Broadway

famous theater district in New York City

65 He enjoyed fame and reveled in the applause of his audiences. He returned to his home in New Orleans to become King Zulu on Mardi Gras day. To this day, he remains the most beloved son of his hometown. The New Orleans airport is named for him.

70 Louis overcame poverty, indignity, and prejudice to become the most famous jazz musician in the world. When he died in 1971 in New York City, 25,000 people came to pay their respects. Together, Louis and jazz made a permanent mark on American culture.

Adapted from *Cobblestone*, "Growing Up With Jazz" by Carol Gelber, © by Carus Publishing Company. Reproduced with permission.

improvisation

creating music as it is being played

Scat and Improvisation

75 What makes jazz jazz? Scat. Improvisation. Where did they come from? Some say that one day Louis Armstrong forgot the words to the song that his band was recording. That accident helped to make him famous and helped make jazz jazz.

80 It was 1926. Louis' band, The Hot Five, was recording. The tune was "Heebie Jeebies," a song about a popular dance. Louis sang the first verse as it was written. "I got the heebies, I mean the jeebies . . . come on and do that dance they call the heebie jeebies

85 dance." When he got to the second verse, he sang, "Deep-dah-jeep-bop-a-dobby-oh-doe-dah, leep-a-la-da-dee-da-dee-oh-bo."

The story goes that he had dropped the sheet music and could not remember the words. He did not
90 want to spoil the master. (The master was the wax cylinder used to press recordings.) To compensate, he made up sounds to go along with the music!

Armstrong did not invent this kind of singing, called scat, but he was one of the first to record it.
95 People loved the funny song. It sold 40,000 copies in just a few weeks. (This was more than many early records sold in their lifetimes.) His records and performances skyrocketed in popularity. Awestruck jazz fans delighted in the fascinating
100 way Armstrong could play around with words and music. Other musicians imitated him, and Louis' style—improvisation—became an element of jazz.

Adapted from *Odyssey*, "Scat and Improvisation" by Virginia A. Spatz, © by Carus Publishing Company. Reproduced with permission.

©Louis Armstrong House & Archives at Queens College/CUNY

Think About It

1. What city was the home of Louis Armstrong?

2. What two ways did he earn money as a child in New Orleans?

3. What might have happened to his life if he had not been sent to reform school?

4. After Louis Armstrong became famous, he returned to New Orleans, his hometown. Why do you think he returned? Do you think you will visit the place where you grew up when you are an adult? Why or why not?

5. What accident helped to make Louis Armstrong famous?

6. When Louis Armstrong forgot the words to the song he was singing, he chose to continue by singing nonsensical words. Why do you think he chose to continue rather than quit?

THE DUKE JAZZES NEWPORT

It was the final night of the 1956 Newport Jazz Festival. The Duke Ellington **Orchestra** came on stage around midnight. Ellington seemed annoyed that people were beginning to leave. He growled, "What are we, the

5 animal act, the acrobats?" He was referring to the old days of vaudeville when less important acts closed shows.

Ellington's fame and the fame of other great jazz musicians had faded. Pop, bebop, and rock and roll had replaced jazz music. Jazz nightclubs had closed, and jazz

10 record sales had plummeted. In 1949, one music critic had suggested that the Ellington era was over. He asked, "Isn't it about time the Ellington orchestra was **disbanded**?" The Duke was one of the greatest musicians of the century. He felt **devastated**.

15 The band played several numbers that night. Finally, Ellington turned from the **piano**. He called for "Diminuendo and Crescendo in Blue," which his orchestra had first recorded in 1937. The band played for a while and then Paul Gonsalves stood up with his

20 **tenor saxophone**. He made his way to the front of the band stand. Ellington encouraged him from the piano, while Jo Jones, who was Count Basie's drummer, cheered him on by beating the rhythm with a newspaper.

Gonsalves started out playing very quietly and softly.

25 Gradually, the loudness of his horn increased. People sat up straighter as excitement began rippling through the crowd. Hot jazz notes soared, and the night began to feel electric. Everybody began to clap. People shouted, and a few danced in the aisles. Soon, the whole audience was on

30 its feet. Gonsalves "blew the joint down" with a solo that went on for 27 **choruses**.

Photographers ran here and there trying to capture the mood on film. The place was wild with excitement, and some even feared a riot. One man asked Ellington to

35 stop, but the band refused. They played for 90 minutes that night and left the audience buzzing. *Down Beat*

orchestra
a large group of musicians playing different instruments

disbanded
stopped functioning as a group; broke up

devastated
extremely upset

piano
a large musical instrument with a keyboard

tenor saxophone
a wind instrument that plays a lower range of notes

choruses
sections of a song played repeatedly

magazine reported that "The final night of the 1956 Newport Jazz Festival will not soon be forgotten."

The Duke's picture made the cover of *Time* magazine. 40 The picture was a symbol for what the music world already knew: Duke Ellington was back.

Adapted from *Cobblestone*, "Making a Statement at Newport" by Brandon Marie Miller, © by Carus Publishing Company. Reproduced with permission.

Think About It

1. What happened when Duke Ellington's band came on stage?

2. This article says that by 1956, Ellington's fame and the fame of other great jazz musicians had faded. What had been the replacements of jazz?

3. What instrument did Paul Gonsalves play in Ellington's band?

4. As Paul Gonsalves played, "people sat up straighter as excitement began rippling through the crowd." What other kinds of events can cause similar excitement in an audience?

5. One man asked Ellington to stop playing because he feared a riot. Defend Ellington's decision to continue playing. Do you think this was a good decision? Why or why not?

6. Explain how you think Duke Ellington felt when he went on stage at the 1956 Newport Jazz Festival. How did he feel when he left the stage that night?

It's Toxic

Toxic Pollutants

**Toxic pollution is everywhere. What can we do about it?
Rachel Carson raised awareness about toxic pollution.
Maybe you can too.**

TEACHER: Let's pretend to interview, or have a conversation with, a
famous person. This individual was one of the first people to
realize the effects of pesticides on our land. Let's have our guest
introduce herself.

STUDENT: I am Miss Rachel Carson.

TEACHER: Miss Carson, I understand you were born and raised on a farm.
Your mom and dad had 65 acres in the state of Pennsylvania.
You must have had quite a time exploring nature.

STUDENT: It was fantastic. The plot of land we had was vast. I was fond of it.

TEACHER: I know that you studied hard in school. How did you learn so
much about nature and the land around you if the information
wasn't in your books?

STUDENT: My Mom and I explored the land. We got facts about rabbits
and rats. We got to track them on the land. We got facts on
plants too. In the pond, we could spot bass and frogs.

TEACHER: When your mom asked what you wanted to be when you grew
up, do you remember what you told her? You said . . . ?

STUDENT: I plan to be a writer.

TEACHER: I understand you enjoyed magazines as a youngster. In fact, your
first article was published in the magazine *St. Nicholas*. This
first article came from stories your older brother told you about
his experiences in the war. Once you submitted the story, you
didn't hear from the publisher for over a year. What did you keep
telling yourself?

STUDENT: They will print facts about combat because the past matters.

TEACHER: When you went to college, you loved your classes, especially biology and English. You had a memorable experience on one of your biology field trips when your teacher taught you to split apart layers of rock. Can you tell us how you found a fossil of a fish?

STUDENT: I split the rock, and it had the imprint of a fish in it.

TEACHER: So you found a fossil, and that fascinated you! I believe you were surprised that you enjoyed the labs as much as the outdoor classes.

STUDENT: The labs had an impact on me.

TEACHER: After you graduated, a friend wrote you a letter that caused you to investigate the use of pesticides. Your friend asked an important question. What question led to your research into the poisons the chemical companies were selling?

STUDENT: What can kill robins?

TEACHER: Your friend had found 14 dead robins in her yard after a poison, or toxin, called DDT had been sprayed to kill bugs. You researched this use of pesticides and found them harmful. What did you plan to do?

STUDENT: I had plans to fix the impact of DDT.

Carson exploring tide pools, Maine, 1955.

Unhatched Ibis eggs, damaged because of DDT pesticide on the Texas Gulf.

TEACHER: As your ideas became accepted, people everywhere wanted to hear you speak and wanted to get to know you better. You didn't like all this fame. Can you tell us why?

STUDENT: I admit I was a bit timid.

TEACHER: But in spite of your timid personality, you felt the need to get the information out to people. How did you overcome your timidity?

STUDENT: The grim facts prompted me to act.

TEACHER: In addition, you decided to write another book. You had already published three books about the sea. The success of these books led you to a realization. What conclusion did you reach about your discovery of how harmful DDT is?

STUDENT: My job was to print the facts.

TEACHER: Can you summarize some of your advice from the book that was printed?

STUDENT: We must stop the quick profit from DDT. The land is vast, but the damage to the land is drastic. The task is to stop toxins.

TEACHER: Many people criticized your book and said your information was false. In response to this, President John F. Kennedy asked for a special report from scientists to find out which side was right. What was the conclusion?

STUDENT: They said toxins can kill, and toxic pollution is bad.

TEACHER: In this selection, we will look at how some of our behaviors, both as individuals and as a population, impact this world in which we live. Our topic is toxic pollution and how it affects our planet. What is our topic?

STUDENT: The topic is pollution. It is toxic. Toxins have a drastic impact on the land.

TEACHER: Pollution is caused when people act in a careless or irresponsible way. They forget the pressing need to keep the Earth's environment clean. For example, instead of reusing and recycling items, people throw them away. These items often end up in a landfill. Landfills require more and more space. They also make the surrounding land less desirable. What will happen when we have too much garbage?

STUDENT: Landfills have a limit. They will fill up. Vast tracts of land will be bad.

TEACHER: People need to find ways to change their behavior. Disposable products are convenient but they are not good for the environment. What can people do?

STUDENT: They can stop and think. They can limit bad habits.

TEACHER: Think of all the small things some people drop every day without thinking: bottles, caps, and drink cans. These are all examples of litter. Littering pollutes the immediate environment. Tell me two ways people litter.

STUDENT: They drop cans and caps.

TEACHER: When people camp out and picnic, they need to make sure they have picked up all of their trash. They need to leave the area clean and natural, just as they found it. Tell me two areas that need to be left clean.

STUDENT: Camps have to be clean, and picnic spots have to be clean.

TEACHER: Individuals and families in the nation and the world have environmental responsibilities. The goods we produce are needed, but the cost to the environment must also be considered. Consumers need to make the environment a priority. What can consumers do?

STUDENT: They can act and insist on a clean environment.

TEACHER: One group that must answer the call to be responsible is farmers. Farmers till the land and plant crops. What is their job?

STUDENT: They till the land and plant crops.

TEACHER: We need the goods that farmers produce. Farmers need us to buy their produce. To make more profit, some farmers use pesticides and fertilizers to make their crops grow more quickly. This puts the individual farmer at odds with the environment. Tell me about the farmer's conflict.

STUDENT: He has a conflict about profit and loss.

TEACHER: Let's look at an example of how the farmer contributes to pollution. Think of a farm on a hilltop. Where is the farm?

STUDENT: The farm is on a hilltop.

TEACHER: Often, farms are also beside rivers and ponds. The soil is usually better in these areas. When a farmer fertilizes his crops, that substance ends up in the soil. Some of the fertilizer is absorbed by the plants. Some of it is washed into the river or pond by rain. What happens to the fertilizer that is not used by the plants?

STUDENT: It spills off the hilltop and into the water.

TEACHER: When this happens, it sets off a sequence of events that causes pollution. The small green plants in the water are fertilized and grow faster than they normally would. This causes water plants to become thick on the top of the water and block light. The plants use up gases, like oxygen. Then fish, such as bass, cannot get the gases they need to live. In the end, all the bass in the lake die. Why did the bass die?

STUDENT: The plants got oxygen, but the bass did not.

TEACHER: Pesticides are chemicals that kill bugs, and herbicides are chemicals that kill the weeds in fields. These toxins are also washed into rivers or ponds by the rain. They kill the plants and animals living in the water. Frogs, bass, and moss may die as a result. Explain how a toxic chemical affects life in and beside the water.

STUDENT: Toxins kill frogs, bass, and moss.

Rainfall washes fertilizers and toxic pesticides into rivers and streams.

TEACHER: Paraphrase what I say. Large factories, or plants, also dump toxic chemicals into our fresh water supply. These toxins contribute to pollution in the environment. Rainfall washes fertilizers and toxic pesticides into rivers and streams.

STUDENT: Big plants drop toxins into the environment.

TEACHER: The final pollutant to discuss is something we take for granted every day. When we go places, our cars consume gas. Not all of the gas is used. Paraphrase this sentence: "Cars, trucks, and vans emit leftover particles as a form of pollution."

STUDENT: The gas is from traffic, and traffic gas is pollution.

TEACHER: This form of pollution is called smog. What is it?

STUDENT: It is smog.

TEACHER: Smog is like a heavy mist that hangs over a city. It pollutes the air. What is smog?

STUDENT: Smog is a toxic mist.

TEACHER: There are several ways we can begin to solve the problem of pollution. First, we need more information. Information can be provided in classes and clinics. What can we do?

STUDENT: We have clinics, and they can give facts.

TEACHER: Second, we need laws, or bills, that make those who pollute responsible.

STUDENT: How can we pass bills?

TEACHER: Informing the public and our lawmakers is important. Paraphrase these ideas.

STUDENT: We can insist on passing the bills. We can take a stand and act. We can have an impact.

Rachel Carson

Rachel Carson's love of nature changed the world. She was born on a farm in Pennsylvania in 1907, so she felt close to nature from an early age. At first, she thought she would be a writer, but then she decided to
5 be a scientist. She graduated from college and wrote a book about life in the sea called *The Sea Around Us*. Her writing was powerful. She taught the public to look at nature in a new way.

After World War II, Carson bought a house on
10 the coast of Maine to be close to the sea. One day, a friend told Carson that her property had been sprayed with DDT to kill mosquitoes. Soon after, her friend had found 14 songbirds dead. She washed out the birdbath, but it didn't get rid of the DDT. Carson felt
15 that she must do something. She had to warn people about the dangers of pesticides. At that time, the U.S. government approved the use of pesticides. They killed weeds and harmful insects. They helped more crops to grow. But Carson knew that they killed friendly insects
20 too. Bees were needed to **pollinate** the fruit trees, and spraying killed the bees. To convince people, she would

pollinate
to carry pollen from one plant to another

have to do some careful research. She worked for many years on writing and rewriting her book. She got sick with cancer, but she kept on working.

25   Finally, her book was published in 1962. She called it *Silent Spring*. What did the title mean? It **predicted** a terrible time. The book opened with a description of a beautiful town. When a fine, white powder was sprayed from the sky, the town fell silent. There were

30 no birds singing. Carson warned that people should not try to **control** nature. Carson said that trying to have nature work for us could lead to trouble. We didn't know what could happen in the future. She said that the destruction of any part of the web of life could

35 threaten the human race. Carson said, "We need to think of ourselves differently. The universe is vast. It is incredible. We are just a tiny part of it."

    Millions of copies of the book sold. Many would **criticize** Carson's book. They accused her of being a

40 sentimental bird watcher who would rather see crops die and people go hungry than kill a few birds. Many more people agreed with her, however. They demanded the U.S. government do something. President John F.

predicted
to have told about something ahead of time

control
to have power over; to hold back

criticize
to point out problems or faults with someone or something

Rachel Carson wrote her manuscript for Silent Spring *by hand.*

Kennedy appointed a group of people to investigate the
45 use of pesticides.

Carson won many awards for her work to **protect**
nature. She died in 1964, and eight years later, the
U.S. government banned the use of DDT and some
other chemical pesticides. It also created an **agency**
50 to protect the environment. Rachel Carson was ahead
of her time. She knew that songbirds would no longer
sing in the spring unless people stopped polluting the
environment. As a writer and a scientist, she changed
the way many people look at the planet Earth. In 1970,
55 people celebrated the first Earth Day. Today, many think
the world is a better place because of Rachel Carson.

protect
to keep safe

agency
an official group that
is in charge of
certain laws and
rules

Adapted from *Appleseeds*, "Rachel Carson's World of Wonder"
by Sylvia Salsbury, © by Carus Publishing Company.
Reproduced with permission.

Rachel Louise Carson

Born: May 27, 1907, in Springdale, Pennsylvania

Died: April 14, 1964, in Silver Spring, Maryland

Books: Under the Sea-Wind (1941), The Sea Around Us (1951),
The Edge of the Sea (1955), Silent Spring (1962), and
The Sense of Wonder (posthumous, 1965)

Answer It
Say the answer in a complete sentence.

1. How do pesticides harm living things?
2. What did Rachel Carson warn people about?
3. How did Rachel Carson warn the world about pesticides?
4. Why did Rachel Carson choose the title *Silent Spring*?
5. Why is the world a better place because of Rachel Carson?

Coming Clean About Toxic Pollution

Toxic Waste

Toxic waste spoils everything. It destroys our land, water, air, plants, and animals. A toxic substance, even a small amount, can harm plant or animal life. Where does toxic waste come from? It can come from
5 factories that make a wide range of products. It can come from pesticides sprayed on the land or in the water. When we throw things away, toxic substances get buried in our landfills. When it rains, toxic pollutants in the ground are washed into lakes, rivers,
10 and the ocean. We are all at risk from **toxins** in our environment.

Air Pollution

Air supplies us with **oxygen**, which we need to live. When we put toxic substances into the air, we breathe those into our lungs as well. What happens when the
15 air is polluted? We breathe in poison. We breathe in harmful gases and fumes. We can't always see the pollution. Sometimes, we see it as a dirty mist called

toxins
poisons

pollution
harmful things put into the air, water, or land

oxygen
a gas that people and animals need to live

Emissions from power plants react with sunlight and moisture to create acid rain.

fumes
unhealthy gases or smoke

device
a machine or tool that has a special use

acid rain
rain that contains chemicals harmful to plants and animals

smog. The **fumes** that come from cars and trucks make smog. Most modern cars have a **device** called
20 a catalytic converter. This device treats the exhaust before it leaves the car, removing harmful substances.

Acid Rain

How is acid rain created? Air pollution combines with water in the air to create rain containing acid. Gases that come from vehicles and power plants make
25 acid rain. When acid rain falls, it can kill plants on land and fish in lakes and streams. It can eat away at stone. Statues and buildings start to crumble.

River Pollution

How do rivers get polluted? There are many toxins in our homes. These include paint thinner, cleaning
30 supplies, bug spray, and fertilizer. When toxins are washed down the drain, they get into our sewers and eventually our rivers. If these toxins are buried in landfills, the rain can flush them into rivers. There, they harm the fish and other forms of life.

Sea Pollution

35　　Many of the toxic substances produced on land end up in the ocean. When waste pours into the sea, it may be eaten by small fish. Then bigger fish and sea animals feed on those fish. The toxins build up to dangerous levels. The effects of pollution on sea life
40　and shore wildlife can be terrible. We can't think of the ocean as a place to dump our waste.

Dead Lakes

　　Do you know what a dead lake is? A dead lake doesn't have any fish. How does this happen? Pollution falls into the lake. The pollution can make water plants
45　like algae grow rapidly. The algae block the sunlight. They use up all the water's oxygen. Fish and other water animals die. A dead lake can't support a variety of life.

Your Responsibility

　　We all need to do our part to protect our
50　environment from toxins. What can you do to help?

Answer It
Say the answer in a complete sentence.

1. How does toxic waste spoil everything?

2. What happens when the air is polluted?

3. How is smog made?

4. How does acid rain harm the environment?

5. Where do toxins come from?

Riddle of the Frogs

The discovery of abnormal frogs led to questions and research that may make a big difference in our understanding of how we can affect our world.

In 1995, a group of Minnesota students was
5 enjoying a science class outing. However, on a nature walk, they saw something shocking—weird frogs. They looked like sensational creations out of a Hollywood screenwriter's imagination, yet they were real. Some had just one hind leg. At first, the students thought they had
10 stepped on them and hurt them. Then they saw frogs with three or more hind legs. One frog had two feet on one of its hind legs. Over half the frogs the students found were **deformed**.

The students recorded what they saw in their
15 notebooks. They returned and took pictures. What caused this? they asked. Could it be pesticides or **fertilizers**? The students contacted local scientists, and they wrote to the Minnesota Pollution Control Agency.

Their discovery launched the Minnesota New
20 Country School Frog Project. Scientists began examining frogs too. Deformed frogs were found in Oregon, Delaware, Canada—many other locations. Experts judged the phenomenon threatening; it indicated something was amiss. Scientists were
25 **alert**. They applied their knowledge of nature and

deformed
disfigured, misshapen

fertilizers
substances that increase plant production

alert
keenly attentive, observant

biology. The students had the opportunity to learn from and assist scientists all over the country. The scientists taught them how to keep accurate track of the frogs and test the water for chemicals.

30   The students were doing essential work, and they felt proud. What if they hadn't **discovered** the frogs? Serendipity—a lucky accident—had led to the discovery, but it was their work that produced important results. One student said, "If you try...you can make a difference 35 in your town, your city, or even your country."

    Today, we have laws that **ban** dangerous toxins. The deformities remain both a riddle and an opportunity for further learning. Numerous possible factors could have damaged the frogs. Scientists and students have much 40 more research to do!

    Rachel Carson was a biologist who sounded the first loud alarm about the fragile nature of the **environment** with her book *Silent Spring;* she would have been proud of these students. She, too, understood 45 the interdependence of all living creatures—whether we have two legs, four, or even one, we all depend upon each other, and our environment depends on all of us.

discovered
learned through observation; realized

ban
to forbid or prohibit

environment
everything that surrounds and affects the lives of living things

Adapted from *Appleseeds*, "The Riddle of the Frogs" by Judy Rosenbaum, © by Carus Publishing Company. Reproduced with permission.

Think About It

1. When and where did the students find the strange-looking frogs?

2. What was strange about the frogs the students saw?

3. What was the name of the project that began as the result of the students' observations?

4. The students found deformed frogs on their field trip. What other types of animals could have been affected by toxins in the environment? Why?

5. One student said, "If you try . . . you can make a difference in your town, your city, or even your country." What are some ways that you can help preserve the environment?

6. Why do you think these students were proud of their work? Why did they think their work was important?

AMAZON Toxins

Schultes and Makuna boys take shelter at the falls of Yayacopi, Río Apaporis.

One determined scientist ventured into the jungle, learned the ways of others, and repeatedly braved deadly disease—all for a plant. But the mysterious leaf he sought may be a medical miracle and yet another potent
5 symbol of humanity's need to save the rainforests.

In 1941, Richard Schultes went to Columbia, South America, where he saw a tiny orchid. He pressed it between the pages of his passport. It was the first of more than 25,000 plants he would collect.

10 But finding one type of vegetation in particular would become his greatest quest. He traveled to the northwest **Amazon** area to identify plants used to make toxins known as curare (pronounced kȳoo-rä'rä). Richard found the best toxin makers in the Amazon—
15 the Kofan people. Though they lived a **primitive** lifestyle, they knew more than anybody else about Amazon toxins.

To learn about Amazon toxins, Richard had to understand the Kofan people. In the Kofan language,
20 *medicine* and *poison* equal the same word. *Poison* means "death to an animal." *Medicine* means "death to a disease."

The latter use interested other scientists. Could toxins have medical value? Curare caused **paralysis** .

Amazon
a rain forest in South America

primitive
simple, non-industrial

paralysis
inability to move one's body parts

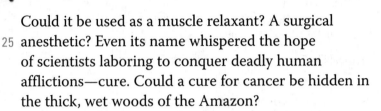

Could it be used as a muscle relaxant? A surgical
25 anesthetic? Even its name whispered the hope
of scientists laboring to conquer deadly human
afflictions—cure. Could a cure for cancer be hidden in
the thick, wet woods of the Amazon?

So, the National Research Council sent Richard to
30 gather the plants. With the Kofan medicine man, he
prepared curare for study. To make curare toxins, the
Kofan use a woody vine from the moonseed family.
They scrape off the bark. Then, they pour water over it
and collect and boil the drippings. Then, they remove
35 the scum. Last, they apply it to the tips of darts and
arrows. Richard learned that the Kofan know the
differences between plants. Every one has his own
curare recipes. There are individual recipes for each
animal and bird.

40   To preserve **specimens** , Schultes invented a new
method. In the old method, plants were dried with heat.
Unfortunately, that made the leaf **brittle** . Instead, he
dipped specimens in alcohol or formaldehyde. Then,
they were laid between sheets of paper.

specimens
individual items in
a group; samples

brittle
easily breakable

*The Kofan people use darts
and arrows dipped in curare.*

malaria

an infectious disease spread by mosquitoes

45   For the sake of science, Richard almost sacrificed his safety and health. He suffered repeated attacks of **malaria**. He even came down with beriberi, from a lack of vitamins. Often, those calamities required that he be hospitalized.

50   Today, the Amazon rainforest is shrinking. Native cultures are disappearing. Now more than ever, science needs to rescue plants. The Amazon people know the mysteries and powers of plants. It is urgent that we retain that knowledge!

55   With new technology in medicine, "nature becomes more important, not less important," Mark J. Plotkin concludes. Mark works for the Amazon Conservation Team in Arlington, Virginia. "Finding new and useful plants is the key to understanding."

60   The history of Amazonian toxins is still being written. Could you be its next explorer—and help discover a cure?

Adapted from *Appleseeds*, "Hunting for Poisons" by Bernice E. Magee, © by Carus Publishing Company. Reproduced with permission.

Think About It

1. Where did Richard Schultes go?

2. What is *curare* (kyo͞o-rä'rā)?

3. Schultes improved upon the old method of preserving plant specimens. Describe the difference between the old and the new methods of preservation.

4. Why do you think that people like Richard Schultes are willing to risk their lives for science? Think of other professions that involve risking one's own life. Are you interested in any of those professions?

5. Richard Schultes came down with beriberi as a result of not getting enough vitamins. Why do you think he had difficulty getting enough vitamins?

6. The Amazon rain forest is shrinking because the land is being cleared for other uses. How do you think Schultes would feel about this? Why?

Resources

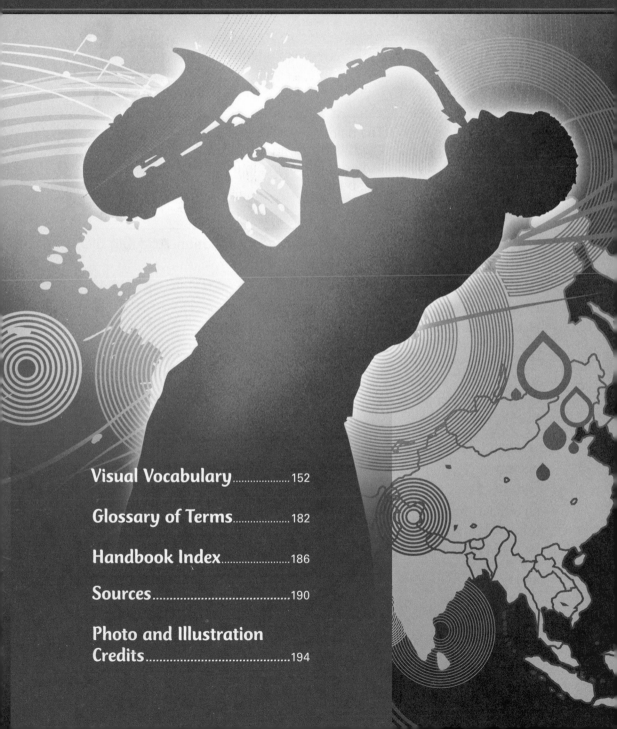

Visual Vocabulary

a

(ā) *article*

any; one

I have a pear.

abstraction

(ăb-străk′shən) *noun*

art that doesn't look like a real object

The painting was an abstraction. It did not look like people playing in a jazz band.

acid rain

(ăs′ĭd rān) *noun*

rain that contains chemicals harmful to plants and animals

Acid rain is caused by pollution. Acid rain kills plants and animals.

affects

(ə-fĕktz′) *verb*

causes a change; has an impact on

The wind affects how the kite flies. Stronger winds make the kite fly higher.

agency

(ā′jən-sē) *noun*

an official group that is in charge of certain laws and rules

The United States has an agency that works to keep the air, water, and Earth safe and clean.

alert

(ə-lûrt′) *adjective*

keenly attentive, observant

The deer was alert for danger.

Amazon

(ăm'ə-zŏn') *noun*

a rain forest in South America

Many types of plants and animals live in the Amazon.

are

(är) *verb*

a form of *be*; used with *you*, *we*, or *they*

1. You are happy.
2. We are running.
3. They are the best team.

associated

(ə-sō'sē-āt'ĕd) *verb*

related, connected

She was associated with others who wanted to protect the environment.

astronauts

(ăs'trə-nôtz') *noun*

people trained for space flight

The astronauts worked in space.

aware

(ə-wâr') *adjective*

watchful of or knowing about

You need to be aware of cars when you cross the street. You need to look both ways.

Visual Vocabulary

B

ban
(băn) *verb*
to forbid or prohibit

Many states ban cigarette smoking in public places.

barren
(băr'ən) *adjective*
without plant life; unproductive

The moon is a barren place.

bat colonies
(băt kŏl'ə-nēz) *noun*
groups of bats living together

We saw bat colonies living in the caves.

be
(bē) *verb*
to exist

Be happy. Do not be sad.

bold
(bōld)
1. *noun* darkened letters or words
2. *adjective* easily seen, flashy

1. We knew the word was important because it was in **bold**. The letters in the word were darker.
2. I painted flowers using **bold** colors. I used bright red, orange, and yellow.

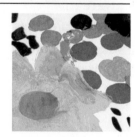

borders

(bôr′dərz) *noun*

lines that mark the edge of an area

A map of the United States has borders. The borders are drawn around the states.

---

brilliant

(brĭl′yənt) *adjective*

very bright; giving off lots of light

The sun is very bright. It gives off a brilliant light.

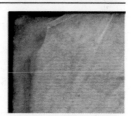

---

brittle

(brĭt′l) *adjective*

easily breakable

The pages of the old book were brittle.

Broadway

(brôd′wā′) *noun*

famous theater district in New York City

We saw a play on Broadway when we visited New York City.

---

bronchitis

(brŏn-kī′tĭs) *noun*

an infection of the tubes that lead to the lungs

The doctor says my bad cough is caused by bronchitis.

---

bugle

(byo͞o′gəl) *noun*

a trumpet-shaped horn without keys

The man played a song on the bugle.

Visual Vocabulary

call (kôl) **and response**
(ənd rĭ-spŏns′) *noun*

a singing or speaking style where one person or group sings or says something and another group answers by singing or saying something

The team players did call-and-response before the game. The coach said, "Who will win?" The team said, "We will win."

carriage
(kăr′ĭj) *noun*

a horse-drawn vehicle with wheels

When we went to New York, we took a carriage ride through Central Park.

choruses
(kôr′əs-əz) *noun*

sections of a song played repeatedly

There were many choruses in the musical performance.

circumnavigate
(sûr′kəm-năv′ĭ-gāt′) *verb*

to go all the way around; circle

Early explorers wanted to circumnavigate the world.

civil engineers
(sĭv′əl ĕn′jə-nîrz′) *noun*

people who design and build public bridges, highways, and other structures

Many civil engineers worked on the Big Dig.

Columbus

(kə-lŭm'bəs) *noun*

famous Italian explorer

Columbus sailed to America.

combat

(kŏm'băt') *noun*

having to do with a fight or battle

When soldiers go to war, they are in combat.

complex

(kəm-plĕks') *adjective*

complicated, intricate

The spider web had not been disturbed and was very complex.

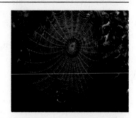

constellation

(kŏn'stə-lā'shən) *noun*

a group of stars that form a shape

The Big Dipper is a constellation. Its stars make the shape of a spoon in the sky.

continent

(kŏn'tə-nənt) *noun*

a major landmass

The United States is on the continent of North America.

control

(kən-trōl') *verb*

to have power over; to hold back

My dog likes to run. I use a leash to control him.

Visual Vocabulary

criticize

(krĭt'ĭ-sīz') *verb*

to point out problems or faults with someone or something

Some people criticize the factory for polluting the air.

---

culture

(kŭl'chər) *noun*

the language, customs, and beliefs of a group of people

Traveling is a good way to learn about a different culture.

D

---

debate

(dĭ-bāt') *noun*

formal discussion or argument

The class was divided as to which book was better, so the teacher held a debate so students could argue their points.

---

deformed

(dĭ-fôrmd') *adjective*

disfigured, misshapen

The frog had three legs and was deformed.

---

desert

(dĕz'ərt) *noun*

a dry place with little rainfall

There was no water in the hot, sandy desert.

devastated

(dĕv'ə-stāt'əd)

adjective

extremely upset

The family was devastated when their house burned down.

---

device

(dĭ-vīs') *noun*

a machine or tool that has a special use

A can opener is a device. So is a pencil sharpener.

---

disbanded

(dĭs-bănd'əd) *verb*

stopped functioning as a group; broke up

The group disbanded when one member moved away.

---

discovered

(dĭ-skŭv'ərd) *verb*

learned through observation; realized

Scientists discovered a new animal in the rainforest.

---

distinct

(dĭ-stĭngkt') *adjective*

clearly different from others; worth noticing

Tom's painting is distinct. It does not look like anyone else's.

---

distortion

(dĭ-stôr'shən) *noun*

imperfect view

The distortion in the mirror made people look like they had funny shapes.

Visual Vocabulary

do

(do͞o) *verb*

1. used to ask questions

2. to cause to happen

1. Do you want grapes or an orange?
2. The students do their homework. I do the dishes.

---

does

(dŭz) *verb*

1. present form of *do*; used with *he, she,* or *it*

2. used to ask questions

1. He does a dance.
2. Does she dance?

---

down

(doun) *adverb*

a lower place

They are going down to the first floor.

---

dragons

(drăg'ənz) *noun*

mythical, winged monsters

The fairy-tale was about knights fighting with dragons.

E

---

emerges

(ĭ-mûrj'əz) *verb*

comes out of; appears

The sun is behind a cloud. Then the sun emerges from behind the cloud.

environment

(ĕn-vī′rən-mənt) *noun*

everything that surrounds and affects the lives of living things

It is important to take care of our environment.

---

eroded

(ĭ-rōd′əd) *adjective*

worn away

The eroded dirt road was closed to traffic.

---

exaggerated

(ĭg-zăj′ə-rāt′əd) *verb*

overstated or magnified

She exaggerated her story by saying the fish was larger than it was.

F

---

famous

(fā′məs) *adjective*

having widespread recognition

George Washington was famous because he was the first president of our country.

---

fertilizers

(fûr′tl-ī′zərz) *noun*

substances that increase plant production

Dad put fertilizers on our grass to make it grow.

for

(fôr) *preposition*

1. in order to have, keep, or get
2. intend to give to
3. because of

1. He asked for a burrito.
2. This is for you.
3. He got a prize for winning.

---

fossils

(fŏs'əlz) *noun*

the bones or the marks left by animals and plants from a long time ago

People find fossils in rocks. The fossils show what leaves and animals looked like long ago.

---

foundations

(foun-dā'shənz) *noun*

supportive bases on which buildings stand

The foundations of the buildings were built first. They were made of concrete.

---

fragile

(frăj'el) *adjective*

easily broken; delicate

The fragile egg broke when it fell off the table.

---

frail

(frāl) *adjective*

weak, sickly

My grandpa is 90 years old. He is frail.

from

(frŭm) *preposition*

out of, coming
out of

I am from Los Angeles. He is from New York.

frontier

(frŭn-tîr′) *noun*

an area that is
being explored

People went west to explore
the frontier.

fumes

(fyōōmz) *noun*

unhealthy gases
or smoke

The fumes from the truck
made me sick.

G

gravity

(grăv′ĭ-tē) *noun*

natural pull between
celestial bodies

The moon's orbit is affected
by the Earth's gravity.

H

he

(hē) *pronoun*

referring to any male

He is a boy.

He

She

Visual Vocabulary

her
(hər)

1. *pronoun* referring to any female
2. *adjective* belonging to a female

1. Give the pencil to her.
2. Her name is Mary.

---

here
(hîr) *adverb*

in or at a close place

Here is a ruler.

---

honored
(ŏn'ərd) *verb*

respected, admired

Police and firefighters are honored in our country.

---

how
(hou) *adverb* **or**
conjunction

asks the question in what way

How do I do this?

I

I
(ī) *pronoun*

used to refer to oneself

I am Joe.

Iceland

(īs'lənd) *noun*

an island nation in the North Atlantic

Early explorers sailed to Iceland.

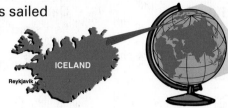

---

ignorance

(ĭg'nər-əns) *noun*

lack of knowledge

I did not know what the man was saying because of my ignorance of Spanish.

---

immortal

(ĭ-môr'tl) *adjective*

something or someone that will never die

No human being is immortal.

---

improvisation

(ĭm-prŏv'ĭ-zā'shən) *noun*

creating music as it is being played

When the piano player forgot his song, he used improvisation instead.

---

indicated

(ĭn'dĭ-kāt'əd) *verb*

served as a sign of something; showed

The dark clouds indicated a storm was coming.

---

inspires

(ĭn-spīrz') *verb*

causes a person to do something

My brother plays music. He inspires me to play too.

Visual Vocabulary

interfere

(ĭn′tər-fîr′) *verb*

to get in the way of; disturb

Dams can interfere with fish swimming in rivers. They can get in the way of fish swimming up rivers.

---

intriguing

(ĭn-trēg′ĭng) *adjective*

very interesting; fascinating

Outer space is very intriguing to me.

---

is

(ĭz) *verb*

a form of *be*; used with *he*, *she*, or *it*

He   She is   It is

1. He is a boy.   2. She is a girl.   3. It is a cat.

K

---

key

(kē) *noun*

a list of symbols used on a map

The key listed the symbol used to show parks on the map.

Interstate	
State Highway	
Water	
Park	

L

---

lakes

(lāks) *noun*

large bodies of still water

Boats can sail across lakes. There are many lakes shown on this map.

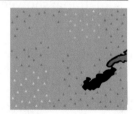

---

landfill

(lănd'fĭl') *noun*

a site where dirt has filled in low-lying ground

Before building, they had to level the site with dirt by making a landfill.

legendary

(lĕj'ən-dĕr'ē) *adjective*

extremely well-known; mythical

Louis Armstrong is a legendary musician.

limits

(lĭm'ĭtz) *noun*

things that prevent something from being perfect or complete

This map has limits because it doesn't show details of the landscape.

llama

(lä'mə) *noun*

a long-haired animal related to the camel

The llama has long hair and can carry heavy loads.

log

(lôg)

1. *verb* to write down what happened

2. *noun* a record of what happened

1. I log how far I run each day.

2. I use a notebook for my log.

Visual Vocabulary

M

malaria

(mə-lâr′ē-ə) *noun*

an infectious disease spread by mosquitoes

In some jungle environments, malaria makes people sick.

---

mammals

(măm′əlz) *noun*

warm-blooded animals

A mouse, a whale, and a human are examples of mammals.

Mardi Gras

(mär′dē grä′) *noun*

a holiday in New Orleans with parades and carnivals

People have fun at Mardi Gras. They can watch a parade.

---

me

(mē) *pronoun*

a form of *I*; word used to refer to oneself

This is a photo of me.

---

merchant

(mûr′chənt) *noun*

a person who buys and sells things for a living

My father owns a lamp shop. He is a merchant.

---

mesas

(mā′səz) *noun*

wide, flat-topped hills

There are many mesas in the southwestern United States.

mood

(mōōd) *noun*

the feeling created by something

You can be in a happy mood or a sad mood.

---

mortal

(môr′tl) *adjective*

something or someone that will die someday

Castor was mortal, and Pollux was immortal. Castor would die, and Pollux would live forever.

---

negligence

(nĕg′lĭ-jəns) *noun*

lack of care; lack of concern

The flower died because of my negligence. I was careless about watering it.

New Orleans

(nōō ôr′lənz) *noun*

a city in southeastern Louisiana

People like to visit the city of New Orleans. It has the Mardi Gras.

New Orleans

Niger

(nī′jər) *noun*

a country of west Africa

The Touareg people live in Niger.

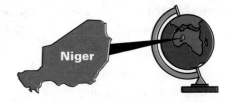

Niger

---

nominations

(nŏm′ə-nā′shənz) *noun*

names of people to be picked for a job or award

We need to pick someone to be the president of our club. We have three nominations.

Visual Vocabulary

Norway
(nôr′wā′) *noun*
a country of
Northern Europe

Norway is a beautiful country that is cold in the winter.

---

now
(nou) *adverb*
at the present time

I ate breakfast this morning.
I am eating lunch now.

---

of
(ŭv, ŏv, əv) *preposition*
belonging to

I am a member of the team.

---

opera
(ŏp′rə) *noun*
a play set to music

We went to an opera. The actors sang their parts.

---

orchestra
(ôr′kĭ-strə) *noun*
a large group of
musicians playing
different instruments

The orchestra had many musicians.

---

overhaul
(ō′vər-hôl′) *noun*
a large repair job;
renovation

The truck needed an overhaul after the long road trip.

---

oxygen

(ŏk'sĭ-jən) *noun*

a gas that people and animals need to live

Air has oxygen. People and animals need to breathe oxygen to live.

---

paralysis

(pə-răl'ĭ-sĭs) *noun*

inability to move one's body parts

As a result of the accident, she had paralysis in her legs. She couldn't walk.

---

piano

(pē-ăn'ō) *noun*

a large musical instrument with a keyboard

I play the piano when I get home from school.

---

plains

(plānz) *noun*

large, flat areas of land without trees

We could see for miles across the flat plains.

---

plantations

(plăn-tā'shənz) *noun*

large farms or areas of land

Bananas are grown on plantations.

---

poets

(pō'ĭtz) *noun*

writers of verse

The poets wrote poems. They read their poems aloud.

pollinate

(pŏl'ə-nāt') *verb*

to carry pollen from one plant to another

Bees carry pollen from one flower to another. They pollinate plants.

---

pollution

(pə-lōō'shən) *noun*

harmful things put into the air, water, or land

Pollution in the lake is killing the fish.

---

ponds

(pŏndz) *noun*

small bodies of still water

Ducks swim on ponds in the park.

---

porous

(pôr'əs) *adjective*

having many small holes or pores

A sponge is porous.

---

predicted

(prĭ-dĭkt'əd) *verb*

to have told about something ahead of time

It was cloudy. I predicted it would rain.

---

prefer

(prĭ-fûr) *verb*

to choose a more desirable option

I prefer chocolate ice cream over vanilla.

primitive

(prĭm´ĭ-tĭv) *adjective*

simple, non-industrial

Some people in the Amazon live a primitive life.

---

prized

(prīzd) *adjective*

treasured, valued

Her baseball cards are her prized possession.

---

prolific

(prə-lĭf´ĭk) *adjective*

having large amounts; abundant

Information is prolific on the Web.

---

proposed

(prə-pōzd´) *adjective*

suggested

The proposed new ballpark would be built on the north side of town.

---

prosperity

(prŏ-spĕr´ĭtē) *noun*

financial success

He wished for prosperity as a result of his hard work.

---

protect

(prə-tĕkt´) *verb*

to keep safe

Seat belts protect us. They keep us from getting hurt.

Visual Vocabulary

R

realized

(rē'ə-līzd') *verb*

came to understand;
sensed

I realized she was right.

---

recipe

(rĕs'ə-pē') *noun*

a list of steps and parts
needed to make food
or something else

He used a recipe to make the
cookies. The recipe told how
to mix the flour, eggs, and
butter.

---

remarkable

(rĭ-mär'kə-bəl) *adjective*

worth noticing;
special or uncommon

Will won first prize for his
remarkable art. It was very
special. We all were talking
about it.

---

rhythm

(rĭth'əm) *noun*

a regular pattern,
such as beats
in music

The beat of the drum sets the rhythm of
the music.

---

rivers

(rĭv'ərz) *noun*

large streams of
flowing water

Two rivers flow through the
town. The rivers are wide
and deep.

said

(sĕd) *verb*

to have spoken something

Miguel said "Hello" in English and "Hola" in Spanish.

Hello, Hola.

satellites

(săt'l-ītz') *noun*

objects in space that go around planets to get facts

Satellites orbit the Earth. They take pictures of the Earth and outer space.

scenario

(sĭ-nâr'ē-ō') *noun*

an outline of expected events

In the best-case scenario, she would graduate from high school and go on to college.

sediment

(sĕd'ə-mənt) *noun*

a dirt-like substance consisting of tiny pieces of rock

The flood deposited thick sediment over the road.

she

(shē) *pronoun*

referring to any female

She is a girl.

He

She

shrines

(shrīnz) *noun*

sacred or spiritual places

People go to shrines to pray.

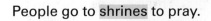

Visual Vocabulary

sneer

(snîr) *noun*

a disrespectful smile; smirk

As he spoke disrespectfully, he had a sneer on his face.

---

sonar

(sō'när') *noun*

ways to locate objects using sound; echolocation

The crew on the ship used sonar to find the sunken ship. The sound waves showed where the sunken ship was located.

---

specimens

(spĕs'ə-mənz) *noun*

individual items in a group; samples

Scientists carefully collect specimens for research and look at them under a microscope.

---

stars

(stärz) *noun*

large objects in space that look like points of light in the night sky

I like to look up at the stars on a dark night.

---

stern

(stûrn) *adjective*

grim, uninviting

The stern policeman wrote me a ticket.

---

strikes

(strīkz) *noun*

failures to hit pitched balls

Three strikes and you're out!

surveys

(sûr′vāz′) *noun*

studies using special tools to find the size and shape of areas of land

The surveys show how large the farm fields are.

telegram

(těl′ĭ-grăm′) *noun*

a message sent by a code-making machine

My grandmother used to send me a telegram on my birthday. Now she sends me an e-mail instead.

telepathic

(těl′əpăth′ĭk) *adjective*

communicating through means other than senses

My friend is telepathic because she often knows what I am thinking.

tenor saxophone

(těn′ər săk′sə-fōn′) *noun*

a wind instrument that plays a lower range of notes

She plays a tenor saxophone in the band.

that

(thăt) *pronoun*

used to show something that is farther away

That is a book.

Visual Vocabulary

the

(thə) *article*

a certain thing

 The owl

 The boy

 The girl

1. The owl flies. 2. The boy smiles. 3. The girl waves.

---

theory

(thîr′ē) *noun*

idea or explanation not proven scientifically

The scientists came up with a theory to help explain how stars are formed.

---

there

(thâr) *adverb*

in or at a farther place

There is a ruler.

 Here is a ruler.

 There is a ruler.

---

these

(thēz) *pronoun*

used to show multiple things that are closer

These are pens.

 These are pens.

 Those are books.

---

they

(thā) *pronoun*

used to refer to a group being spoken or written about

They are biking.

---

this

(thĭs) *pronoun*

used to show something that is closer

This is a pen.

 This is a pen.

 That is a book.

---

those

(thōz) *pronoun*

used to show multiple things that are farther away

Those are books.

These are pens.

Those are books.

---

to

(tōō) *preposition*

1. for or about a thing
2. toward something
3. word used with verbs to indicate doing something

1. She had a key to the gate.
2. He went to the park.
3. I like to sing.

---

toxins

(tŏk'sĭnz) *noun*

poisons

The toxins from the factory got into the water and made people sick.

U

uncomfortable

(ŭn-kŭm'fər-tə-bəl) *adjective*

feeling discomfort

My shoes are too small. They are uncomfortable.

V

vast

(văst) *adjective*

very large, immense

The ocean is vast.

virtue

(vûr′chōō) *noun*

moral excellence, goodness

One important virtue is honesty. It is good to tell the truth.

 W

---

waifs

(wāfs) *noun*

abandoned children; orphans

Hopefully, the waifs in the school will find a good home.

---

was

(wŭz) *verb*

to have been in the past; used with *I, he, she,* or *it*

I was asleep when the telephone rang.

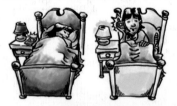

---

we

(wē) *pronoun*

the group which includes the speaker

We are biking together as a group.

---

were

(wûr) *verb*

to have been in the past; used with *you, we,* or *they*

They were outside. Then they went inside.

---

what

(hwŭt) *pronoun*

a question word asking which thing or things

What is that?

when

(wĕn) *adverb*

asks the question:
at what time?

When is the bus coming?

where

(wâr) *adverb*

asks the question:
in what place?

Where is my shoe?

who

(ho͞o) *pronoun*

asks the question:
what person
or people?

Who is at the door?

why

(wī) *adverb* **or**
conjunction

asks the question:
for what reason?

Why are you crying?

Y

you

(yo͞o) *pronoun*

used to show the
person being
spoken to

You are
Mary.

You are Mary.

your

(yôr) *adjective*

belonging to the
person you are
talking to

Your eyes are brown.

Book A contains these terms. Unit numbers where these terms first appear follow each definition.

Adjective. A word used to describe a noun. An adjective asks which one? how many? or what kind? A prepositional phrase may also be used as an adjective. Example: *Six new kids from the school won the big game.* (Unit 6)

Adverb. A word used to describe a verb. An adverb answers the questions when? where? and how? A prepositional phrase can also be used as an adverb. Examples: Julio ran **yesterday**. *Julio ran in the park. Julio ran quickly.* (Unit 4)

Antonym. A word that means the opposite of another word. Examples: *above/below*; *dead/alive*; *happy/sad*. (Unit 2)

Apostrophe. A punctuation mark that shows singular possession. Examples: *the man's map* (the map that belongs to the man); *Ann's pan* (the pan that belongs to Ann). (Unit 2)

Attribute. A characteristic or quality, such as size, part, color, or function. Examples: *A windmill is tall. A windmill has a base and blades. Windmills are narrow. Windmills catch wind energy to make electric energy.* (Unit 5)

Capital letters. Uppercase letters used at the beginning of all sentences. Examples: **T**he cat sat. **W**here did it sit? **I**t sat on my lap! (Unit 1)

Comma. A punctuation mark used to signal a pause when reading or writing to clarify meaning. Examples: *At the end of the song, Jim clapped. Yesterday, school was cancelled.* (Unit 5)

Compound word. A word made up of two or more smaller words. Examples: *sandbag, hotdog, catnip.* (Unit 3)

Consonant. A closed sound produced using airflow restricted or closed by the lips, teeth, or tongue. Letters represent consonant sounds. Examples: *m, s, t, b*. (Unit 1)

Direct object. A noun or pronoun that receives the action of the main verb in the predicate. Answers the question: Who or what received the action? Example: *Casey visits granddad.* (Units 3, 4)

Doubling rule. A spelling rule that says to double a final consonant before adding a suffix beginning with a vowel when (1) it's a one-syllable word, (2) it has one vowel, and (3) it ends in one consonant. Examples: *hopping, stopping.* Also called the 1-1-1 Rule. (Unit 6)

Expository text. Text that provides information and includes a topic. Facts and examples support the topic. Also called informational text and nonfiction. Example: "Batty About Bats!" (Unit 1)

Idiom. A common phrase that cannot be understood by the meanings of its separate words—only by the entire phrase. It cannot be changed, or the idiom loses its meaning. Example: *hit the sack* = go to bed; *pat on the back* = congratulate. (Unit 4)

Informational text. Text that provides information and includes a topic. Facts and examples support the topic. Also called expository text and nonfiction. Example: "Batty About Bats!" (Unit 1)

Nonfiction. Text that provides information and includes a topic. Facts and examples support the topic. Also called informational text. Example: "Batty About Bats!" (Unit 1)

Noun. A word that names a person, place, thing, or idea. Examples: *bat, fact, cab.* (Unit 1)

Noun, abstract. A word that names an idea or a thought that we cannot see or touch. Examples: *love, Saturday, sports, democracy.* (Unit 3)

Noun, common. A word that names a general person, place, or thing. Examples: *man, city, statue.* (Unit 3)

Noun, concrete. A word that names a person, place, or thing that we can see or touch. Examples: *teacher, car, pencil.* (Unit 3)

Noun, proper. A word that names a specific person, place, or thing. Examples: *Mr. West, Boston, Statue of Liberty.* (Unit 3)

Object of a preposition. A noun or pronoun that ends a prepositional phrase. Examples: *in the **cab**, during the **game**.* (Unit 4)

Phrase. A group of words that does the same job as a single word. Examples: *in the house, with a bang.* (Unit 4)

Plural. A term that means more than one. Nouns are usually made plural by adding **-s**. Examples: *bats, acts, cabs.* (Unit 1)

Possession, singular. One person or thing that owns something. Adding **'s** (apostrophe and the letter <u>s</u>) to a noun signals singular possession. Examples: *Stan's stamps, the van's mat, the man's cap.* (Unit 2)

Predicate. One of two main parts of a sentence. It contains the main verb of the sentence. Example: *The man ran.* (Unit 2)

Preposition. A function word that begins a prepositional phrase. Examples: *at, in, from.* (Unit 4)

Prepositional phrase. A phrase that begins with a preposition and ends with a noun or a pronoun. A prepositional phrase is used either as an adjective or as an adverb. Examples: *in the van, on Monday, to the class.* (Unit 4)

Pronoun. A function word used in place of a noun. Examples: *I, you, he, me, they.* (Unit 4)

Pronoun, nominative (subject). A function word that takes the place of the subject noun in a sentence. Examples: *I, you, he, she, it, we, they.* (Unit 4)

Pronoun, object. A function word that takes the place of the object of a preposition or a direct object. Examples: *me, you, him, her, it, us, them.* (Unit 6)

Punctuation. Marks that indicate the ending of a sentence (period, question mark, and exclamation point), a pause within a sentence (comma), or possession (apostrophe accompanied by the letter <u>s</u>). Examples: *The cat sat. Where did it sit? It sat on my lap! Yesterday, school was cancelled. Sam's map.*

Sentence. A complete thought that contains a subject and a predicate. Examples: *The cat sat. The players talked. Sam acted.* (Unit 1)

Sentence, simple. A complete thought that contains one subject and one predicate. Examples: *The man ran. Casey batted. The bird hopped.* (Unit 2)

Singular. A word that means one of something. Examples: *bat, act, cab.* (Unit 1)

Subject. One of two main parts of a sentence. The subject names the person, place, thing, or idea that the sentence is about. Examples: ***The man*** *made a map.* ***The map*** *helped the man.* (Unit 2)

Syllable. A word or word part that has one vowel sound. Examples: *map, bend, ban • dit.* (Unit 3)

Synonym. A word that has the same meaning as, or a similar meaning to, another word. Examples: *big/large*; *slim/thin*; *mad/angry*. (Unit 3)

Tense, past. A verb that shows action that is finished. Examples: *batted, jogged, sat*. (Unit 4)

Tense, present. A verb that shows action that is happening now. The **-s** at the end of a verb signals present tense. Examples: *hops, drops, stops*. (Unit 4)

Tense, present progressive. A verb form that indicates ongoing action in time. The **-ing** ending on a main verb used with **am**, **is**, or **are** signals the present progressive. Examples: *I* **am sitting**. *She* **is picking**. *We* **are sitting**. (Unit 5)

Verb. A word that describes an action (*run, make*) or a state of being (*is, were*) and that shows time. Examples: *sits* (present tense; happening now), *is fishing* (present progressive; ongoing action), *acted* (past tense; happened in the past). (Units 1, 4, 5)

Verb, helping. A secondary verb that comes before the main verb in a sentence. Forms of **be** can be used as helping verbs when used with different personal pronouns to achieve subject-verb agreement in sentences. Examples: *I* **am** *packing.* *You* **are** *packing. He* **is** *packing.* (Unit 5)

Vowel. An open sound produced by keeping the airflow open. Letters represent vowel sounds. Examples: *a*, *e*, *i*, *o*, *u*, and sometimes *y*. (Unit 1)

idioms, defined, H20

informal outlines, H55

informational text, H47

-ing, adding, H17, H32

IVF topic sentence, H59

k, ways to spell, H14

listening and reading comprehension,
   H46–H50

main ideas, H50

multiple meanings for words, H18

multiple-choice questions, answering, H49

narrative text, H46

nominative (subject) pronouns, H37

nonfiction, H47

nouns
   abstract, H25
   adding -s to, H16
   adding 's to, H18
   common, H25
   concrete, H25
   defined, H24
   as direct objects, H28
   forms of, H26
   functions of, H27–H29
   multiple meanings, H18
   as objects of prepositions, H29
   plural, H16, H26
   proper, H25

   singular, H16, H26
   singular possessive, H18, H26
   as subjects, H27

number
   topic sentences, H60
   words, H60

object pronouns, H38

objects of prepositions, H29

organizing information, H54
   for effective writing, H64, H65, H67
   graphic organizers for, H54
   informal outlines for, H54

paragraphs. *See* writing paragraphs

plural nouns, H16, H26

predicates
   defined, H33
   expansion with adverbs, H43
   expansion with direct object, H42

prepositional phrases, H36

prepositions, H36
   defined, H36
   objects of, nouns as, H29
   showing relationship, H36

present progressive verbs, H17, H32

present tense verbs, H31

pronouns
   defined, H37
   object, H38
   subject (nominative), H37

pronunciation keys
   consonants, H8
   vowels, H8

proper nouns, H25

V

v, words with, H14

verbs
    adding -ing to, H17
    adding -s to, H17
    be, correct use of, H32
    defined, H30
    forms of, H31–H32
    functions of, H33
    as predicates, H33

    present progressive form, H17, H32
    present tense, H31
    singular present tense, H17
    tense timeline, H31

vocabulary and morphology, H16–H23. *See also* compound words
    adding -ing (present progressive), H17
    adding -s (plural noun), H16
    adding -s (singular present tense verb), H17
    adding 's (singular possessive nouns), H18
    antonyms, H21
    attributes, H22
    idiomatic expressions, H20
    meaning parts, H16–H18
    multiple meanings for words, H18
    singular nouns, H16
    synonyms, H21

voice and audience awareness, H64, H65, H67

vowels (v). *See also* consonants (c)
    chart of, H7
    defined, H5
    doubling rule, H15
    pronunciation key, H8
    sound of, number of syllables and, H10, H11–H12
    vc/cv pattern words, H11
    vc/v pattern words, H12

W

word choice, H64, H65, H67

words
    compound, H13
    multiple functions of, H39
    multiple meanings of, H18
    transition, H61

writing
    Blueprint for Writing, H51
    checklist for Book A, H65
    effective, six traits of, H64, H65, H66–H67
    expanded summary, H53
    graphic organizers for, H54
    informal outlines for, H54
    organizing information, H54, H64, H65, H67
    sentences, stages of, H56–H57
    structure of, H51
    summary of, H52–H53

writing paragraphs, H58–H63
    checklist for Book A, H65
    conclusion, H58, H63
    conventions of, H64, H65, H67
    editor's marks and, H66
    E's (explanations, examples, evidence), H58, H62
    ideas and content, H64, H65, H67
    organizing information, H54, H64, H65, H67
    parts of paragraphs and, H58
    revising and, H66–H67
    sentence fluency, H64, H65, H67
    six traits of effective writing and, H64
    supporting details, H58, H61
    topic sentences, H58, H59–H61
    transition words, H61
    voice and audience awareness, H64, H65, H67
    word choice, H64, H65, H67

Unit 1

At Bat

Hechtkopf, Jacqueline. 2002. "At Bat," adapted from *Cricket* (August 2002) © 2002 Carus Publishing Company, 315 Fifth Street, Peru, IL 61354. All rights reserved. Reprinted with permission.*

Bats in China

Kern, Stephen J. 1988. "Bats in Chinese Art." *Bats*, vol. 6, no. 4. Austin, TX: Bat Conservation International, Inc.

Batty About Bats!

Kowalski, Kathiann M. 1999. "Batty About Bats!" adapted from *Odyssey* (March 1999) © 1999 Carus Publishing Company, 315 Fifth Street, Peru, IL 61354. All rights reserved. Reprinted with permission.*

Casey at the Bat!

McGovern, Patrick. "The Baseball Scorecard," http://www.baseballscorecard.com/casey.htm (accessed March 2, 2003).

Unit 2

Atlas: A Book of Maps

Rosenbaum, Judy. 1999. "The Story of Atlas," adapted from *AppleSeeds* (January 1999) © 1999 Carus Publishing Company, 315 Fifth Street, Peru, IL 61354. All rights reserved. Reprinted with permission.*

Floki: Sailor Without a Map, a Norse Myth

Rosinsky, Natalie M. 1999. "Here Be Dragons," adapted from *AppleSeeds* (January 1999) © 1999 Carus Publishing Company, 315 Fifth Street, Peru, IL 61354. All rights reserved. Reprinted with permission.*

The Hardest Maps to Make

Kushner, Sherrill. 1999. "Oceans: Mapping Earth's Last Frontier," adapted from *AppleSeeds* (January 1999) © 1999 Carus Publishing Company, 315 Fifth Street, Peru, IL 61354. All rights reserved. Reprinted with permission.*

A Map Is a Sandwich

Miller, Jeanne. 1999. "A Map Is a Sandwich," adapted from *AppleSeeds* (January 1999) © 1999 Carus Publishing Company, 315 Fifth Street, Peru, IL 61354. All rights reserved. Reprinted with permission.*

Mapping the Unknown

Microsoft ® Encarta ®; Online Encyclopedia. 2003. "Dragon," encarta.msn.com © 1997–2003 Microsoft Corporation. All rights reserved.

Rosinsky, Natalie M. 1999. "Here Be Dragons," adapted from *AppleSeeds* (January 1999) © 1999 Carus Publishing Company, 315 Fifth Street, Peru, IL 61354. All rights reserved. Reprinted with permission.*

Unit 3

Africa Digs

Laliberte, Michelle. 2000. "Finding the Pieces…and Putting Them Back Together Again," adapted from *Odyssey* (September 2000) © 2000 Carus Publishing Company, 315 Fifth Street, Peru, IL 61354. All rights reserved. Reprinted with permission.*

The Big Dig

Belluck, Pam and Katie Zezima. "Accident in Boston's Big Dig Kills Woman in Car." *New York Times*. July 12, 2006. http://www.nytimes.com/2006/07/12/us/12tunnel.html?ex=1310356800&en=f19f993722c72777&ei=5088

*See page 193.

CBS Broadcasting Inc. 2006. "Big Dig Is A Big Mess." July 14, 2006. http://www.cbsnews.com/stories/2006/07/14/cbsnews_investigates/main1806639.shtml.

Massachusetts Turnpike Authority. 2007. "Project Background." http://www.massturnpike.com/bigdig/background/index.html.

Murphy, Sean and Andrew Ryan. "Fast-drying epoxy used in Big Dig let bolts slip over time." *Boston Globe*. July 10, 2007. http:// www.boston.com/news/globe/city_region/breaking_news/2007/07/epoxy_used_in_b.html.

Reuters. 2007. "Adhesive blamed in Boston Big Dig tunnel collapse." July 10, 2007, http://www.reuters.com/article/domesticNews/idUSHO08389120070710?feedType=RSS.

Toupin, Laurie Ann. 2002. "Big Dig," adapted from *Odyssey* (September 2002) © 2002 Carus Publishing Company, 315 Fifth Street, Peru, IL 61354. All rights reserved. Reprinted with permission.*

Dig This!

IvyRose Ltd. 2007. "Calcite." http://www.ivy-rose.co.uk/Crystals/Calcite.htm.

Kornegay, Shureice. 2000. "Fantastic Journeys: Dig This!" adapted from *Odyssey* (September 2000) © 2000 Carus Publishing Company, 315 Fifth Street, Peru, IL 61354. All rights reserved. Reprinted with permission.*

Unit 4

Conjoined Twins

Annas, George J. 1987. "At Law: Siamese Twins: Killing One to Save the Other."

The Hastings Center Report, Vol. 17, No. 2 (Apr., 1987), pp. 27-29. http://links.jstor.
org/sici?sici=0093-0334(198704)17%3A2%3C27%3AALSTKO%3E2.0.CO%3B2-C (accessed August 4, 2007).

Chichester, Page. 1995. "A Hyphenated Life," *Blue Ridge Country*, (November/December), http://www.blueridgecountry.com/newtwins/twins.html (accessed August 4, 2007). Adapted with permission.

Steinmetz, Rabbi Chaim. 2003. "Separating Conjoined Twins." http://www.jlaw.com/Commentary/cojoinedtwins.html (accessed August 4, 2007).

Tankala, Varun. *Conjoined Twins*, http://www.conjoined-twins.i-p.com.

Wikipedia. "Twin." 2007. http://en.wikipedia.org/wiki/Twin.

Gemini: The Twins

Peoria Astronomical Society. 2002. "Gemini," www.astronomical.org/constellations/gem.html.

Raasch, Rick. 1998. "The Constellation Gemini: The Twin Brothers," *The Constellation Home Page*, ed. Edward P. Flasphoehler Jr., The American Association of Amateur Astronomers, www.corvus.com/con-page/winter/gem-01.htm.

Remarkable Twins

Dunn, Marcia. 1999. "As Pilot Prepares to Fly, His Double Helps Out, But Doesn't Step In." STS-103, *Houston Chronicle's* Space Chronicle (May 2), www.chron.com/content/interactive/space/missions/sts-103/stories/990502.html.

Elvis Presley Enterprises, Inc. 2003. "All About Elvis," biography from Elvis Presley: The Official Website, www.elvis.com/elvisology/bio.

*See page 193.

Sanders, Craig. 1999; 2003. "Twin Portraits: Twins in Outer Space," Twinstuff.com (April; February), www.twinstuff.com/twinnasa.htm.

———. 1999. "Twin Portraits: The Twin Wranglers," Twinstuff.com (May), www.twinstuff.com/wranglers.htm. Used with permission of Kim and Kari Baker.

Naming Pluto's Tiny Twin Moons

BBC News. 2005. "Two new moons found around Pluto." November 1, 2005. http://news.bbc.co.uk/1/hi/sci/tech/4396546.stm (accessed September 14, 2007).

Britt, Robert Roy. 2006. "Scientists Decide Pluto's No Longer a Planet." http://www.msnbc.msn.com/id/14489259/ (accessed August 4, 2007).

International Astronomical Union. 2005. "Welcome." http://www.iau.org/HOME.2.0.html (accessed August 4, 2007).

Klotz, Irene. 2006. "Pluto's Tiny Twin Moons Named." Discovery News. http://dsc.discovery.com/news/2006/06/22/plutomoon_spa.html?category=space (accessed August 4, 2007).

NASA. 2006. "Hubble Essentials." Space Telescope Science Institute (STScI). http://hubblesite.org/the_telescope/hubble_essentials (accessed August 4, 2007).

———. 2006. "Pluto's Two Small Moons Officially Named Nix and Hydra." June 22, 2006. Space Telescope Science Institute (STScI). http://hubblesite.org/newscenter/archive/releases/2006/29/full/ (accessed September 14, 2007).

Science@NASA. 2005. "New Moons of Pluto." November 1, 2005. http://science.nasa.gov/headlines/y2005/01nov_moonsofpluto.htm (accessed September 14, 2007).

SpaceRef Interactive Inc. 2006. "Pluto's New Moons Likely Born with Charon; Pluto May Even Have Rings." February 22, 2006. http://www.spaceref.com/news/viewpr.html?pid=19089 (accessed September 14, 2007). All rights reserved.

Unit 5

The Duke Jazzes Newport

Miller, Brandon Marie. 1993. "Making a Statement at Newport," adapted from *Cobblestone* (May 1993) © 1993 Carus Publishing Company, 315 Fifth Street, Peru, IL 61354. All rights reserved. Reprinted with permission.*

Growing Up With Jazz

Gelber, Carol. 1994. "Growing Up with Jazz," adapted from *Cobblestone* (October 1994) © 1994 Carus Publishing Company, 315 Fifth Street, Peru, IL 61354. All rights reserved. Reprinted with permission.*

Spatz, Virginia A. 1994. "Scat and Improvisation," adapted from Cobblestone (October 1994) © 1994 Carus Publishing Company, 315 Fifth Street, Peru, IL 61354. All rights reserved. Reprinted with permission.*

Jazz: The Recipe

Amey, Heather Mitchell. 1983. "Jazz Ingredients," from *Cobblestone* (October 1983) © 1983 Carus Publishing Company, 315 Fifth Street, Peru, IL 61354. All rights reserved. Adapted with permission.*

*See page 193.

Looking at Jazz

Miller, Marc H. 1994. "Looking at Jazz," adapted from *Cobblestone* (October 1994) © 1994 Carus Publishing Company, 315 Fifth Street, Peru, IL 61354. All rights reserved. Reprinted with permission.*

Unit 6

Amazon Toxins

Benders-Hyde, Elisabeth. 2000. *Blue Planet Biomes*. "Curare." http://www.blueplanetbiomes.org/curare.htm.

Magee, Bernice E. 2001. "Hunting for Poisons," adapted from *AppleSeeds* (April 2003) © 2003 Carus Publishing Company, 315 Fifth Street, Peru, IL 61354. All rights reserved. Reprinted with permission.*

Wikipedia. 2007. "Curare." http://en.wikipedia.org/wiki/Curare

Coming Clean About Toxic Pollution

Wadsworth, Virginia Evarts. 1989. "Cleaner Cleaning," adapted from *Cobblestone* (August 1989) © 1989 Carus Publishing Company, 315 Fifth Street, Peru, IL 61354. All rights reserved. Reprinted with permission.*

Marsh, James. 1995. "Yuck! It's Time to Come Clean About Pollution," from *Young Telegraph: Earth Alert*. Copyright 1995 by Two-Can Publishing, an imprint of Cooper Square Publishing. Adapted and reprinted by permission of Cooper Square Publishing, 4501 Forbes Blvd, Suite 200, Lanham, MD 20706.

Rachel Carson

Salsbury, Sylvia. 1999. "Rachel Carson's World of Wonder," adapted from *AppleSeeds* (March 1999) © 1999 Carus Publishing Company, 315 Fifth Street, Peru, IL 61354. All rights reserved. Reprinted with permission.*

Riddle of the Frogs

Dorota. 2006. "What is a Frog?" *Frogland*. http://allaboutfrogs.org/weird/general/whatisfrog.html.

Rosenbaum, Judy. 1999. "The Riddle of the Frogs," adapted from *AppleSeeds* (March 1999) © 1999 Carus Publishing Company, 315 Fifth Street, Peru, IL 61354. All rights reserved. Reprinted with permission.*

Wikipedia. 2007. "Frog." http://en.wikipedia.org/wiki/Frog.

Cover

Jonathan Till

TOC

Unit 1: Mark Kostich. 20–21. Unit 3: ©Corbis Images/PictureQuest. Unit 4: *t.l.* ©Royalty Free/Corbis; *t.r.* Jan Coy; *m.l.* Mark Doliner; *m.r.* ©Getty Images; b.l. Barbara Page. Unit 5: Martin French. Unit 6: ©Royalty Free/Corbis.

Unit 1

Photographs 3: Mark Kostich. 20–21: ©Merlin D. Tuttle, Bat Conservation International, www.batcon.org. 23: ©William O'Conner, Denver Art Museum Neusteter Textile Collection. 25: ©National Baseball Library/MLB Photos via Getty Images. 28: ©Digital Vision.

Illustrations 4–19: Rick Stromoski. 26: Marty Peterson.

Unit 2

Photographs 57: ©Royalty Free/Corbis.

Illustrations 30–45: Jack Hornady. 46–47: ©Eureka Cartography, Berkeley, CA. 49: ©Woods Hole Oceanographic Institution. 51: ©North Winds Picture Archives. 53: ©North Winds Picture Archives. 54: ©2004 Cobblestone Publishing Company, illustrated by Craig Spearing. 58: ©North Winds Picture Archives.

Unit 3

Photographs 59: ©Corbis Images/PictureQuest. 76: ©Paul S. Sereno, courtesy Project Exploration. 77: ©Paul C. Sereno, courtesy Project Exploration. 78: ©Project Exploration. 79: ©1999–2003 Getty Images. 80: bkgd. courtesy of Massachusetts Turnpike Authority Central Artery/Tunnel Project; *t.* ©PhotoDisc. 81: courtesy of Massachusetts Turnpike Authority Central Artery/Tunnel Project. 82: *t.* courtesy of Massachusetts Turnpike Authority Central Artery/Tunnel Project; *b.* courtesy of Massachusetts Turnpike Authority Central Artery/Tunnel Project. 83: ©Gabrielle Lyon, courtesy Project Exploration. 84: ©Paul C. Sereno, courtesy Project Exploration. 86: ©PhotoDisc.

Illustrations 60–75: Steve McGarry.

Unit 4

Photographs 87: *t.l.* ©Royalty Free/Corbis; *t.r.* Jan Coy; *m.l.* Mark Doliner; *m.r.* ©Getty Images; b.l. Barbara Page; b.r. ©Creatas. 89: ©Used by permission, Elvis Presley Enterprises, Inc. 98: ©Used by permission, Elvis Presley Enterprises, Inc. 99: ©Artville 100: bkgd. ©Digital Stock; *b.l. & b.r.* courtesy of National Aeronautics and Space Administration. 102: bkgd. ©Digital Stock. 105: Courtesy of North Carolina Collection, University of North Carolina Library at Chapel Hill. 108–109: bkgd. courtesy of NASA and STScI. 108, 110: Nix and Hydra photo courtesy of NASA and STScI. 109: courtesy of Andrew Steffl. 111: courtesy of NASA Headquarters - Greatest Images of NASA (NASA_HG_GRIN).

Illustrations 93: ©New York Public Library/Art Resource, NY. 95: Rick Geary. 104: Pauline Brown. 109: Steve Clark.

Unit 5

Photographs 123: National Portrait Gallery, Smithsonian Institution/Art Resource, NY ©The Lisette Model Foundation, Inc. (1983) Used by permission./©Art Resource. 124, 127: Courtesy Louis Armstrong House Museum, Queens College.

Illustrations 113: Martin French. 115: ©Getty Images. 117: ©Getty Images. 118: ©Getty Images. 121–122: Stuart Davis, *Hot Still-Shape for Six Colors—7th Avenue Style*, 1940. Oil on canvas. 36 x 44 7/8 in. (91.44 x 113.98 cm). Museum of Fine Arts, Boston. Gift of the William H. Lane Foundation and the M. and M. Karolik Collection, by exchange, 1983. 120. 128: Susan Jerde.

Unit 6

Photographs 131: ©Royalty Free/Corbis. 133: Courtesy of Lear/Carson Collection, Connecticut College. 134: ©George Silk/Time Life Pictures/Getty Images. 137: ©Royalty Free/Corbis. 138: ©Royalty Free/Corbis. 140: Courtesy of the Lear/Carson Collection, Connecticut College. 141: *Silent Spring* by Rachel Carson, ©1962 by Rachel L. Carson. Used by permission of Frances Collin, Trustee. Any electronic copying or distribution of this text is expressly forbidden. 143: ©Dynamic Graphics. 144: ©iStock.com/akiyoko. 148: R.E. Schultes. 149: ©Alison Wright/Corbis.

Illustrations 146–147: Ursula Vernon. 148–150: Ursula Vernon.

Visual Vocabulary

Photographs Alert: ©istockphoto.com/Taso Hountas. Are: ©istockphoto.com/Galina Barskaya, ©istockphoto.com/Nick Free, ©blend images/Punchstock. Associated: ©digital vision/Punchstock. Astronauts: ©Jupiter images. Ban: ©Jupiter images. Barren: ©Jupiter images. Bat colonies: ©Robert Gill; Papilio/Corbis. Be: ©Jupiter images. Bold: ©istockphoto.com/Jorge Delgado. Borders: ©Jupiter images. Brilliant: ©Jupiter images. Brittle: ©istockphoto.com/Brian Powell. Broadway: ©istockphoto.com/Allan Pospisil. Bugle: ©designpics.com/Punchstock. Carriage: ©istockphoto.com/William Roger. Civil Engineers: ©Jupiter images. Columbus: ©pixtal/Punchstock. Combat: ©istockphoto.com/Craig Debourbon. Complex: ©Jupiter images. Constellation: ©istockphoto.com/Dan Mitchell. Continent: ©Jupiter images. Culture: ©istockphoto.com/SpotX. Desert: ©Jupiter images. Device: ©Jupiter images. Distortion: ©Jupiter images. Down: ©istockphoto.com/Kathy Konkle. Dragons: ©Jupiter images. Environment: ©Jupiter images. Famous: ©Jupiter Images. Fertilizers: ©istockphoto.com/James Boulette. Fossils: ©Jupiter Images. Foundations: ©Jupiter Images. Fragile: ©istockphoto.com/Clint Scholz. Frail: ©istockphoto.com/Silvia Jansen. Frontier: ©Jupiter Images. Gravity: courtesy of NASA Headquarters - Greatest Images of NASA (NASA_HG_GRIN). He: ©Jupiter Images. Honored: ©Jupiter Images. Iceland: ©Map Resources. Ignorance: ©Jupiter images. Indicated: ©istockphoto.com/Clint Spencer. Interfere: AArtPack. Lakes: ©Jupiter images. Landfill: ©istockphoto.com/Robert Kelsey. Limits: ©istockphoto.com/Jami Garrison. Llama: ©Jupiter images. Mammals: AArtPack. Mardi Gras: ©istockphoto.com/EauClaire Media. Merchant: ©blend/Punchstock. Mood: ©Jupiter images. New Orleans: ©Map Resources. Niger: ©Map Resources. Norway: ©Map Resources. Opera: ©Image Club/Punchstock. Orchestra: ©Jupiter Images. Piano: ©istockphoto.com/Emiliano Fincato. Plains: ©Jupiter Images. Plantations: ©istockphoto.com/Marco Richter. Pollinate: ©istockphoto.com/Serdar Yagci. Pollution: ©istockphoto.com/Stacey Newman. Ponds: ©Jupiter images. Porous: ©istockphoto.com/Nick Free. Primitive: ©photodisc/Punchstock. Prosperity: ©Image Source/Punchstock. Protect: ©Jupiter Images. Rivers: ©Jupiter Images. Said: ©Jupiter Images. Satellites: ©Jupiter Images. She: ©Jupiter Images. Shrines: ©Jupiter Images. Sneer: ©Jupiter Images. Sonar: ©Woods Hole Oceanographic Institution. Specimens: ©istockphoto.com/Jayson Punwani. Stars: courtesy of NASA and STScI. Strikes: ©istockphoto.com/Amy Myers. Surveys: ©istockphoto.com/Malcolm Romain. Telegraph: ©istockphoto.com/Don Wilkie, ©istockphoto.com/Richard Cano. Tenor Saxophone: ©istockphoto.com/Paul Piebinga. That: AArtPack. They: ©istockphoto.com/Steve Krull. This: AArtPack. Toxins: ©Jupiter images. Vast: ©istockphotos.com/Alexander Hafemann. We: ©istockphoto.com/nikada33.

Illustrations Tom Zilis